Matthew
Jesus Speaks

A Daily Devotional by:
Jeffrey D. Harris
Parted Waters

www.partedwaters.net

Millington, TN

Acknowledgements

In this the second Devotional in my Parted Waters Series, it is a continuation of the encouragements and prayers from so many great friends. At the current count there are 104 members of my Parted Waters Facebook Page, as of July 2012.

The feedback I have received through Email, Facebook©, and actually face to face, have kept me writing. With the number of people requesting a second book, I could do nothing but write it. This is a collection or series I wrote originally for my online semi-daily devotional. I have put them together into this book, with the help and patients of my wife, who waited as I typed away in the other room.

Thank you to my loving wife who helped me with my final editing. She has also dealt with my hours of laptop time. I love my wife.

For more information and more books please visit my web site;
www.partedwaters.net
or join my devotional on Facebook © at "Parted Waters"

Scripture quotations are taken from the *Holy Bible*, New Living Translation, copyright © 1996. Used by permission of Tyndale House Publishers, Inc., Wheaton, Illinois 60189. All rights reserved.

Parted Waters – Jesus Speaks (The Book of Matthew)

In some Bibles the words of Jesus are typed in Red Lettering. So the words Written in Red are the Word's Jesus spoke while he was on the earth as a man. Here I am pointing out just a few of the things Jesus said and talked about. This also only covers the Book of Matthew. Please read along, but don't just read the verses I have pointed out. I urge you to read the entire paragraph or chapter. Read not only the words of Jesus, but also read what was going on. Then I would also say read over the words of Jesus extra carefully.

This Devotional is NOT meant to be a stand alone book. It is meant to be read with your Bible open to the verses selected for each given day. No book, no matter how good a book is, it should never replace your Bible reading. I deliberately have left the verses out of this book, so my readers will open there own Bibles and dig in deeper than even I am take them.

The words contained in this book will encourage you at times, and at other times they will challenge you to be better. Then there will be some days the words will be for someone you know. This is a great opportunity for you to share and help. Not everything from God is for us directly; sometimes it is for us to give away.

God's Word is for us to give away. As we give it away, we are blessed beyond the words.

Read and be Blessed.   Read and Bless others.

Bible 101

Bible Literacy is not as common as one would hope. It's just not taught today. Old Testament, New Testament, What's what? What does King James mean? How is the New King James different? What is Hebrew, Greek, and today's English version? There are a lot of things to know, but who is telling, or teaching? Well I guess I am.

Versions:

There are many different versions of the bible. These versions come in two different styles, Translations and Paraphrased.

Translations: are bibles that have been written as close as possible to the original language. The Original language is not a single language. The two original languages are Greek and Hebrew. The New Testament is mostly Greek. This is because the Greeks were the first to, not only conquer, but unit the known world. Under one government they brought a single currency and language to all the lands they took over. This included Israel. While it's true during the New Testament, it was the Romans that ruled, the Greek language was still used as a unifier.

There are those who claim the King James Version is the only one that should be used. I can not agree. My first thought is about all the people around the world that can't read English. There is no way for them to benefit from God's word.

Jesus himself used the scriptures word for word, but also paraphrased. Of course he can do that it's his words. But all his parables were so the common man could understand him and the kingdom of God. The King James is hard to read. I can't help but believe that Jesus would want us to understand his word. If anything we should all learn Greek if God was that strict. There are Denominations that only read the scriptures in Latin. So the Word of God is of little benefit. It doesn't bring the understanding God's word is promised to give. This has left those denominations desolate. The members have no idea the gospel of Christ, and are left understanding only the tradition of Church, the very thing Jesus spoke out against.

The NIV has been the most popular alternate. New International Version, It is very Good.

I love the New Living Translation. The Amplified Bible is a paraphrased version that puts an emphasis on the words that don't translate directly from Greek to English in one word, so it lists all the words that can be used. I enjoy this version.

The Message is one of the newest paraphrased bibles that is very well done.

Is there a bad translation? YES

There are versions that have left out verses, and reworded versions to say what they want them to say instead of what it was originally. Not by using the word "Great" instead of "Awesome."

How can we tell. I use one key verse. John 1:1-4 & 14.

Here we read in the King James as well as the NIV, New King James, New Living Translation, the Message, The Word, is God, and became Flesh.

Jesus is the word, He is God.

If you wonder about a translation, open it up to John 1, If it does not say "The Word Was God" then it is bad.

The Jehovah Witness version says The Word was A god, insinuating that Jesus was not the God, which conflicts with other references that there is only one God, but it is rewritten that way.

Next is the type of Bibles and Features.

Some come as New Testament, Full Bibles, Reference Bibles, Study Bibles, Narratives, and Devotionals.

It's a bit pricy, but I love my Life Application Bible, which is a study Bible.

I also have a thin line which is smaller in size and easier to carry.

A study Bible has just about everything. Charts, Maps, Notes, Info on People of the Bible, Prophecies and Fulfillments, Dictionary, Concordance, Time Lines, and Synopsis of each book.

Features:

RED LETTER: Red letter is very common, these Bibles have the words of Jesus printed in red. This way you can pick out what Jesus said directly and what other people just say about Jesus. I always wish they had come up with a Bible that has God's words in the Old Testament in Blue.

CHARTS: about everything, most compare things or people. Sins verses Love, six stages of Jesus' trial, Jesus and forgiveness, Days of creation. These charts can add to your knowledge and provide a simple and concise place to review a topic.

DICTIONARY: just as it says, tells about items and people of the bible.

CONCORDANCE: a list of topics, people, words, and where you can find this information about them in the bible. I use this feature the most.

MAPS: usually the last thing in the Bible. They show bible lands, national lines over different time periods, and people movements.

NOTES: the life application has both small notes about key verses on every page, which are found at the bottom of the page. It also has notes about the book and the people that either wrote the book or are key characters in the book. If the book covers decades of time, like 1st and 2nd Kings, the note on People and Places, are found through out the book, but mostly the notes are just before the start of the book.

OLD TESTAMENT: The books of the Bible that where written before Jesus became Flesh. It starts with creation and ending with Malachi and the last of the prophesies nearly 500 years before the birth of Jesus. There are 39 books that make up the Old Testament.

NEW TESTAMENT: The collection of books and letters written about Jesus, starting from his fleshly birth, and ending with the revelations of the end of times. The New Testament is made up of 27 books, most of them letters.

Matthew – Jesus Speaks

The Gospel or "The Good News" (which is what gospel means)

God created us in his image, Body, Soul, Spirit.

He gave us a free will to decide to follow him or to Sin. Since we choose sin, our spirit is separated from God. To reunite our soul and spirit with God, we need to get rid of the sin. We can not do it ourselves. We can't be good enough for Perfection. So that means we can't go to heaven.

The answer should be no, except for one thing. **Jesus**.

Jesus came and paid the penalty for our sin. Our sin is wiped away when and only when we acknowledge and admit our sin.

We must admit we are sinners. Then we need to apologize to God and ask him to take away the sin. Our sin is then erased by Jesus' blood.

We then need to accept Jesus as our Lord, and acknowledge that he is God. We can not accept Jesus as savior without the faith that Jesus is God and the creator.

Remember God is Love and loves us more then we can ever know. He wants us to succeed; he wants all of us to join him in heaven. But he can't let sin in. So we can't do it with out Jesus wiping them out.

The saving faith is Free. Jesus' forgiveness is free; we can't pay for it, or do enough to earn it. We get it free if we ask for the forgiveness.

Jesus wants us to be forgiven. He does. He wants to have you as a friend. He wants a relationship with you.

The Love is ready for you. But you have to repent.

The Good News is repentance is possible and it works.

Christian Basics

All of us believers have an element or two that comes easy. These elements need to be balanced with all the elements.

The Elements are:

Humility / Repentance
Faith / Believe
Read the Word/ Bible
Prayer
Worship
Sharing

It all starts with **Repentance**, and being born again. This Humility needs to be an every day event, for his mercies are new every morning. We must be Humble and Believe that Jesus is God and died for our sins and rose again. For most of us, this is the easy part (For the most part).

Faith comes from the Word of God. (Rom 10:17) To build our faith to a level that is usable, we **must Read** his Word. Reading the Bible on a daily basis is essential to our relationship with Jesus. But again, some find this part very easy. There is no one to talk to and no action that would be uncomfortable.

Pray; Not just over your meal, but pray to God in the manner Jesus told us. (Matt 6) Prayer is not just our needs, it is praying for wisdom, help from sin, and Praise. Pray for God's Will, to be done. We must also, pray for others. This takes thinking about others in our humility. I mean praying, not just from afar, but pray for them while you are with them. Pray with others, just as the early church did as they waited for the Holy Spirit. Some of us are good at praying, it is easy.

Worship, and **Praise;** Worship should be part of everything we do. We also need to vocalize our love for God and his son. We need to say it, we need to sing it, and we need to pray it. This may be the easiest thing to do, but too often not done at all. We can go to church and sing along. We can even sing along with K-Love or our favorite CD.

Sharing our faith; we need to share our testimony, share how God has helped us. Share how God's love has changed our lives. Share how wonderful it is to know Jesus and his Grace. Now this is with out a doubt the hardest part for almost all of us. But with out this element there will not be a next generation of believers. We are all followers of Jesus because someone else shared. Who will you share with?

Can we do them all?
Be humble,
Pray alone, for others, and with others.
Worship him, with our deeds and our voice.
Read the Bible and study how it applies to us.
Share what God is doing and what he has already done.
Believe he is God and can do anything, even for us.

Easier said than done, but oh so worth it.

As my Pastor, Pastor Matt has been telling me. "If we want to see things we have never seen before, we need to do things we have never done before. This maybe all or one of the elements you have been neglecting. Live your life in Christ to the fullest by doing all the elements.

PREFACE

"Written in Red"

The red letters or words printed with red ink, found in many of our bibles are the words that Jesus spoke. These words are recorded by his disciples. I am going to dig into the words that Jesus spoken as remembered and written by the apostle Matthew. Matthew was one of the twelve disciples Jesus hand-picked to start the church after he returned to Heaven. Matthew was with Jesus pretty much from the beginning of his ministry and spent almost ever day with Jesus. He heard the words Jesus spoke with his own ears. He saw the miracles with his own eyes. He felt the touch of God with his own hands.

This devotional is not a look at Matthew's life or even the book of Matthew as a whole. It is a look at what Jesus said as he walked this earth. A look at how he responded to the people that loved him. A look at how he responded to the people who hated him. A look at how he spoke mercy to people that needed him. A look at what he said to the hurting. A look at what he said to instruct and teach his disciples.

More importantly this devotional looks at what Jesus said for us to hear today. There is much to learn from his words and how he reacted to all sorts of situations. Read and be blessed by the words Jesus is speaking to you.

Jesus doesn't speak until chapter 3. This is why I have skipped over chapter 1 & 2.

Day 1

Matthew 3:15 – Jesus' First Words

Matthew 3:15 "It should be done, for we must carry out all that God requires." NLT

This is the first line Jesus speaks in the gospels. As you can see he doesn't say anything until chapter 3. This is because Matthew gives us a pre history of Jesus, including his genealogy, first. Then he tells the story of Christmas. Jesus was a baby not much to record except, "Goo Goo."

In verse 15, we find Jesus standing in front of his cousin John the Baptist. John has known him his whole life, but this is the first time he sees him as God. John being a humble man refuses to baptize the one he was waiting to come and baptize him. He tells Jesus he is not worthy. He does eventually baptize Jesus.

Jesus' reply is our first written in red moment. He is claiming the law and his need to obey every aspect. This is the beginning of a sinless life. Baptism isn't a requirement for salvation, but it is requested by God to do it. Even though it is only a request and not a law, Jesus still stepped up to the river and did it.

Step 1: He shows us that he will be obedient. The first thing he teaches us is Obedience. It must be important. We live under Grace, but we must still be obedient. We don't have to be perfect, but we must try.

Step 2: Immediately after his baptism the Holy Spirit comes down on him.

First he is obedient then he receives the Holy Spirit.
Importance; Jesus needs the Spirit to start his ministry. We have to have the Spirit to move forward in our relationship with Jesus and to carry out our role in his ministry. The Spirit comes in when we repent and believe.

Day 2

Matthew 4:4 – Fight with Words; God's Words

When Jesus was faced with the temptation of the Devil, it wasn't very tempting to Jesus the 'Son of God', but his body (100% Human body) was hungry from his fast. And you know when we get really hungry; we sometimes become "not our selves" or "act unusual."

Try this; skip Breakfast then skip Lunch, then at about 6:00pm, go to the grocery store with a fried chicken place in front of it. Get out of the car, take a deep breath, may be two until you can almost taste the chicken.

Now go in and only get 1 loaf of Bread and 1 gallon of milk.

If you can do it, then you are better than I.

The devil had him right where he wanted him. Weak as he will ever be.

The scripture he used was not a verse that will have much meaning outside of this situation.

The Main Point is that Jesus used God's Word to battle the temptation and the enemy.

If Jesus did it, it must be the best method. So we need to use the scriptures.

When we are faced with tough times, turn to the Bible.

When we are weak spiritually and or physically, turn to the Bible.

Also:

The verse Jesus used is also a reminder that things are not the only thing that keeps us alive.

To live a full life and live it to the max, you need to include the Word of God.

The Bible is the Key to a great life. After all it is all about Jesus.

Day 3

Matthew 4:7 – Faith Without Seeing.

7 Jesus responded, "The Scriptures also say, 'You must not test the LORD your God.'" NLT

Question Him. Ask him why. Plead all you want, but do not dare him or taunt him.

Testing God is if you were to say, "If you are real, then do this..." This isn't an unforgivable sin. Thomas did it when he said that he wouldn't believe until he put his fingers inside the holes in Jesus' hands and side. Jesus let him, and Thomas repented. So it's not the end of the world if you have tried to test God. But it should be something we need to avoid.

True faith believes without seeing. The proof you need to believe in Jesus will come as you seek him in the scriptures. He has made himself real to me over and over again. It is in different ways at different times.

Sometimes it is a thought that you just know came from God and it's the answer to a problem you have been praying for.

Sometimes it's when I type out what I feel the Lord has told me about a scripture, and the Pastor preaches on the same thing that following Sunday.

For you it could be in many different ways. The ways are as different as we are. God has a unique and special way to show himself to each of us. Sometimes it is the same as someone else and God uses that similarity to bond or encourage each other.

God is still just as awesome today as he ever was.

Look for his Love, and learn to Love him back.

Day 4

Matthew 4:10 – Satan's Lies

10 "Get out of here, Satan," Jesus told him. "For the Scriptures say, 'You must worship the LORD your God and serve only him.'" NLT

Sometimes we just have to shout. GET OUT OF HERE!

Here we find Satan offering Jesus the whole world, Duh! He already had it. The devil was still convinced he could trick him into bowing to himself.

How easy is it for man to fall for this trick? It may not be as obvious as Satan talking face to face, but the choice is there.

Do we turn away from God to get what we want? Are God's desires less important to us than our own dreams?

We just want to be happy, is there anything wrong with that?

The answer is yes if you turn away from God and try to find it.

The thing is; the long lasting happiness and joy is already yours. But sometimes we think it could be just a little bit better. So we chase dead ends to find the next big thing. But the truth is, if we draw closer to God and deeper in the Word of God; the joy is beyond what we could ever hope for.

Don't give up what you already have for nothing.

Keep your eyes on Jesus.

When you hear a lie to stray and know in your heart, Yell it out, "Get out of here, I have Jesus and that's better than anything you have to offer."

It may seem crazy, but if it keeps you on the road to glory, do it. What ever you need to do to keep Satan's lies from tricking you, just do it.

Day 5

Matthew 4:17 - Restoration

Obvious the 'repent' part is key to all of our salvation. The focal point of our faith and the first step in the repair and growth of our relationship with God is repentance. A turn away from the pride that says, 'I am good enough' and 'I don't need help.' to the humility of a "I am sort of perfect and I need help." But when I read this verse, it was the second half that caught my attention for the first time.

"The Kingdom of God is near"

I have not given this much thought before past the fact that Jesus is pointing out, that Jesus himself has come into the world. This is the kingdom of God coming to earth. 'The Prince of Peace.'

But if I may; I see more. The kingdom; like the Body of Christ is made up of us, the people that turn to Jesus and become heirs with Christ. With this in mind, I see the restoration of the relationship between Man and God. This restoration at the time of Jesus' comment, hadn't taken place. This is the moment Israel has been waiting for since before Abraham. No more need of a Priest to offer our sacrifices. We can go to God directly in prayer. We can call for forgiveness and repent in Jesus' name. We can have the power and comfort of the Holy Spirit. We can find guidance and direction from the Holy Spirit. We can have the Living God living inside us. All this was right on the horizon.

For those of you who have moved away from your home town. Going home and you pass the last exit before the turn off, and you can see the water tower that has your home town's name on the side; welcoming you. Excitement fills your heart as you know your mom or Dad is just a few miles away, waiting to greet you.

Guess what. We are living in the post restoration time period. We don't have to wait. The time for living in the fullness of God is NOW. The Kingdom of God is no longer near, it is HERE. I am living in it and I am so filled with Joy because of it.

Day 6

Matthew 4:19 – Be Willing. Be Amazing

Come and let me teach you how to use your talents to bring people to me.

Jesus isn't looking for experts. He is looking for people that are willing to learn.

Teachable is way more valuable than knowledge.

For when knowledge runs out, you reach the end. But someone willing to learn can get past obstacles by learning what they need to get past them.

I recently had a guy that came to help me out on a project. It wasn't long before he became almost worthless. I wanted him to use the nail gun. He had never used one, Instead of trying it, he spent precious time explaining how he used screws. This of course, he did at a job that he no longer had. He refused to try. He was very insistent that he knew more. His work did not live up to the claims. I had to replace him. He was not teachable.

God doesn't want people that are smarter than he is. Fact is if we think that we are, we are delusional.

Talk is cheep.
Talk is worthless to God.

He wants people that are willing to get out there and try. Even when they are not really sure what they are doing. God can take that willingness and do amazing things.

God can and will use us, even when I don't have a clue or even if you don't either.

Be Willing. Be Amazing.

Day 7

Matthew 5 : 3 & 4 – Realize our Need

These next groups of passages are from the best sermon teller of all times; Jesus. This is from his famous 'Sermon on the Mount.'
Next to Psalms this is my favorite part of the Bible.

The first section of the sermon is called the Beatitudes. How we should be. It also tells us what a blessing is. True blessings do not come from Wal-Mart.

Verse 3 says *"blessed are the poor."*
This is followed by a key word, "and." And what?
"And realize their need for him." NLT

Realizing the need for him as I have stated before, is step one in the plan of salvation. Salvation places us into the family of God which leads to inheritance. The Kingdom of God is for all of us who call on Jesus for help. This doesn't happen until we realize our need for him.

So the encouragement for those of us, who have been or are still poor, is that this life is only temporary. There are great things ahead. We may have to wait until Heaven to get the full effect of following Jesus. But don't take this as the only way. If you use the talent God has given you, work hard, and follow the lord's leading you can live a full life until then. Don't use this verse to settle back and not try. It's not an excuse. It is an encouragement. Even greater things are ahead.

Great things are ahead.

Day 8

Matthew 5:5 – Humility

5 God blesses those who are humble, for they will inherit the whole earth. NLT

This is where the World's wisdom and God's teaching are complete opposite. If you want to get ahead, you need to be aggressive and do what ever it takes.

God says, if you work hard and don't get a big head because of your success, you will succeed even more. This is actually true.

Who would you rather work with? The one who is good at every task given him, that is better than he claims.
OR
The one who is quick to tell you how good he is, and rarely lives up to his claims.

It's a no brainier.

So, be better than you claim, which means don't claim it just do it.

Don't make claims you can't live up to.

TRUTH: God honors and blesses the Humble in ways that are nothing but miraculous, because of how awesome they are.

Humility equals greatness in God's eye.

Day 9

Matthew 5:7 & 8 - Mercy

7 God blesses those who are merciful, for they will be shown mercy. NLT

More Blessings!

This time, the Blessings come from being Merciful.
Is there any better blessing than to find mercy?
When someone you love shows you mercy or maybe even a boss who gives you a second chance, it's a relief, a blessed relief.

Finding Mercy is common when we call on Jesus. He gives it to us every time. But can we give it?

If we give it, we will get it.
I don't give it enough.
It is horrible, that I don't want to give others a second chance. Actually a second chance is easy, but what about a fifth time? Eight times?   Twenty times?

It is what we are supposed to do. Jesus told us to forgive 70 times 7. Forgive over and over again.

Showing Mercy? I really have to work on this one.
I don't think you can do it without prayer. Prayer has got to be the Key to Forgiveness.

In his mercy which follows our repentance, leads to a pure heart. A pure heart washed by Jesus Christ. With this pure heart we will see God and it will be a blessing not a terror.
To See God, not under judgment, but under Grace.
The Mercy of God is the ultimate Blessing and we will have it and most of us do have it.
The more we give mercy in daily life, the more we will receive when we mess up. And we all know we are really good at messing up.

I need all the mercy I can get.

Day 10

Matthew 5: 9 – Peace Maker

The Blessings keep coming. We have the promise of our top blessing; to see God. The next blessing mentioned takes some work. Verse 9 is our role in peace. Peace makers. This is hard. It doesn't come naturally nor does it come easily. The easy thing to do is agree with the hate and go along with the argument.

If we are with friends and instead of encouraging them to forgive and pray we encourage them to feel the way they feel. We give them justification, and fueling the anger. This does not help them. It makes them feel good for a moment, but the long run it is destructive. Not peaceful.

Maybe we find ourselves at odds with someone. We can get caught up in being right, no matter what the cost may be. Being right can cost more than we can imagine at the time. The quest to be right can last for decades, and be the source of a feud.

Unless they are asking you to renounce your faith in Christ, it may not be worth the trouble of being right.

We must live in the truth. I am not suggesting you live in a lie. What I am saying is; there are arguments that you can win, but with the loss of a friend, loved one, or potential friend. Insisting on winning is a pride issue. Think about it, and then pray about it. Should you say anything more, or should you say nothing. If you are to say something, let it come from the leading of the Holy Spirit. Speaking out of frustration or from passion generally leads to hate.

Peace is hard. It takes the Holy Spirit, prayer, and asking for help. I can do it. I'm not as consistent as I should be. I miss blessings by not being more consistent. But if I can do it anyone can. It's all about taping into the Holy Spirit for strength.

Day 11

Matthew 5: 11 & 12 – Peer Pressure

The biggest fear that Christian in America have is what others will think about them. It looks like from this scripture it hasn't changed a whole lot since the beginning.

This sermon was very early in Jesus' ministry. I can imagine that the few thousand people that came out to hear Jesus, left friends at home who told them exactly how they felt about them going to listen to a homeless man from Nazareth. Still they went and Jesus encouraged them.

If you are put down for Loving God, rewards beyond our dreams await. We may have to wait awhile, but a promise is a promise.

Question:
Do we value the thoughts of the people around us, more than what God can give us?
Do we not believe Jesus will bless us for our faithfulness and our boldness?

Which is worse? It doesn't really matter. Jesus isn't here to Judge. We don't loose our salvation; He isn't going to fire us from ministry.

What happens is we hurt ourselves, and limit how God can use us. Then we miss out on blessings that are far above what we'd get for anything else. Blessings will come for all of our work for Christ. Why limit it for our appearance?

This is something I have to work on. There are people I won't send this too, because I don't want to loose what little friendship we have. Kind of dumb when I say it out loud, but it's true.

Lord helps us to be bold and show your love to everyone.

Day 12

Matthew 5: 13-16 Salt and Light

Salt and Light.

This has been preached about a lot. Jesus is telling us to live out loud. This means; putting ourselves out there for the world to see. Letting our life display the change that the Lord has made in us.

Can people see the change?

Are your actions a true display of who you are in Christ, or who you are in the world?

Verse 16 is not meant to be a display of how great we are, but a display of how much you love God and others.

Everything we do should point to Jesus. That's the whole point of these 4 verses.

Salt makes the food taste better - We need to make work better for others. We need to make life a little better for others.

Light stands out in the Dark. - We need to light the way to Jesus. Be someone that people will go to when the darkness is too much for them.

Lamp stand - Don't hide what God has done for you. Let your Joy shine out. Share your testimony. Let people know how Jesus got you out of the darkness.

Be humble and joyful, point to God in all you do.

Day 13

Matthew 5:17 - 22 – From Law to Love

Verse 17: Jesus sets the record straight. He was not about to tell the people that the unobtainable law was not needed. Just like today, many of them were looking for an easy way out.

Then he turns on those of us who think, "We are OK". They hope they are good enough for something, hopefully good enough for Heaven.
Come on Jesus, you are on a roll. I have agreed with everything you have said up to this point. Bring it home.
Wait. What?
Verse 22: Anger the same as Murder? No way. Is Jesus out of his mind? That can't be right.
There are a lot of things much worse. Besides, if I get mad, but don't do anything about it, how can that be a sin?

The truth is when we get mad, we rarely don't do anything. We may not cause direct harm, but we are going to tell someone all about it, maybe even more then once. Maybe even until we feel everyone has heard about how we have been wronged.

Jesus comes and starts with the Law. The law is in place until God feels it has served its purpose. Then he goes and makes it even harder.

But the fulfillment of the law is coming very soon. Jesus is the completion. He did not come to eliminate it. The law tells us how to live in such a way that brings honor to God and Love to others.

It keeps us humble.
It keeps us on track.

Never think you are good enough. Our righteousness is only good when it comes from Jesus.

He is the perfect righteousness.

DAY 14

Matthew 5:20 – Righteousness not in Law

20 "But I warn you—unless your righteousness is better than the righteousness of the teachers of religious law and the Pharisees, you will never enter the Kingdom of Heaven!

Verse 20 tells us about the saving righteousness that only comes from one place. That place is JESUS.

Unless our righteousness is better than the ones who follow the law alone, you can't get to heaven. The Pharisees followed the Law, or at least their interpretation of the law, they fell way short.

We have learned the Law isn't enough. The law tells us how to live better, but mainly shows us how weak we are.
The saving Grace and Righteousness that we need, only comes from one place. JESUS.

Jesus is our righteousness. He is talking about himself as the source of righteousness. Jesus is the source of a better righteousness. Not only better, it is perfect and perfectly complete, for our every need.

When we say he is all we need. We are not talking about cars and houses. We are talking about our spiritual needs. He can give us our emotional needs. While he can and does provide the physical needs we have. It is our spiritual needs that are so important and need the most attention.
I can work hard and buy a car with money I have earned under my own power. Yes, God gives us our talents and our abilities, but we can do well even if we don't follow God. Success in this world can come to those who do not love God or even acknowledge his existence. We cannot measure our relationship with God by what we have or don't have. Many of the prophets and disciples were poor.
God is not against us being successful, but it isn't a sign of our faith. It is a sign that we have worked hard. When we work hard and acknowledge God we bring him honor.

Day 15

Matthew 5:27-31 - Divorce

Here's a group of verses on adultery and divorce.

All Sin is based in pride, or the desire to have things or people, in this case. It is total selfishness. Jesus speaks on this directly to make it clear he doesn't want it to happen. We are really good at making excuses for sin. Divorce hasn't changed. Even today we have every excuse under the sun. "He doesn't love me any more" "I fell out of love" "we just don't work together any more." "All we do is fight."

The truth is there is usually someone else we are convinced will change our lives. There is no doubt a change will take place. It won't be the better change we hope for. It is a sin that drags someone else into it. If I divorce my wife, I have hurt her for life. I have caused damage to my children that can't be fixed, by any thing I can do. I leave a woman alone, and unable to move forward in the Lord or in life, like she would if I supported her.

Then the Women that I may choose to replace her with, is hurt equally. The feelings of love and desire may feel good for a time, but can my lover and I grow closer to the Lord? Can I move forward in the ministry God has called me to? Probably not.

How can I move forward in the Lord, when I turn my back on what God demands? How can I when I ignore God's wishes for my life? How can I; when I decide that my desires are more important than God' plan? How can I when I am hurting my family?

Divorce is a ministry killer along with the total devastation it inflicts on the family.

If you are already divorced, do not live in condemnation. For Jesus' blood covers all sin. And you can start over. You can be restored. You will be if you turn to God in humility. I merely warn those that maybe thinking about it. God will restore you but you will have to live with the devastation that is left behind.

Day 16

Matthew 5:33-37 - Being Truthful.

Verses 33 thru 37 are all about keeping your word.

It's wrapped up with verse 37 and just says, "I will and then do it."

Are you known for keeping your word? I would hope that I am. Jesus gives a couple of examples of what not to do.

I think it's simple, "Don't make any promises you can't keep."

If we vow to God to do something and then don't fulfill it, you have dishonored God. Besides that, who are we to use God's name to validate what we say? Our actions should be validation enough. That is Jesus' point.

The second thing I thought about when reading these verses, was the use of big terms. People that don't always tell the truth, often feel the need to validate their words with something else.

Examples:
"You don't know how big this is going to be."
"Dad said."
"I was talking to the president."
"Honest."
"Seriously"
"I'm telling you the truth."

If they feel the need to explain that it is actually the truth, it probably isn't. People that are not prone to lying don't point out that they are telling the truth. Liars are constantly trying to convince people that they are telling the truth.

Speak the truth and let the truth stand for itself. If people don't believe us, it does nothing to us. We shouldn't get bent out of shape. We should let our consistency speak for itself.

DAY 17

Matthew 5:38 - 42 - Revenge

Revenge is sweet some say. Actually most say.

There is a belief that if we get the revenge we want that things will be better. No matter how many times we try it, the results are the same. The results of course are not the desired results. The initial feeling can be satisfying, but the fact of the unchanged situation, changes those feelings.

Revenge doesn't change the initial pain that we are looking to vindicate, it is still there. Jesus knows this and is telling us to not cause more pain because of our pain. The pain drives us to want to cause more pain. But we are to move in Love. Even to the ones we don't like.

Revenge is not sweet. It causes more pain and makes restoration impossible. The only real solution is to the pain we feel is restoration. Restoration comes from Jesus and Love. Love is the cause of restoration. Sharing love will bring it.

This does not mean that sharing love will always change the person that caused the pain. It will go a long way in healing you. There are times when sharing the Love means holding your tongue. It doesn't mean you invite them over for Christmas dinner. Express the love with the Holy Spirit's leading. It may be drastic. It may be simple. Forgive. Move on without letting them pull you down.

Avoiding is not a bad thing unless the Holy Spirit is telling you to talk to them. Keeping a distance may be the best way to show love.

Pray from a distance. Don't plot from a distance. I am very good at this. I need to restrain and pray more.

Day 18

Matthew 5:43 - 48 - Difficult Love

43 "You have heard the law that says, 'Love your neighbor and hate your enemy. 44 But I say, love your enemies Pray for those who persecute you! 45 In that way, you will be acting as true children of your Father in heaven. For he gives his sunlight to both the evil and the good, and he sends rain on the just and the unjust alike. 46 If you love only those who love you, what reward is there for that? Even corrupt tax collectors do that much. 47 If you are kind only to your friends, how are you different from anyone else? Even pagans do that. 48 But you are to be perfect, even as your Father in heaven is perfect. NLT

I believe I have covered the topic of loving your enemies. It's what makes us different, or at least we are supposed to act different.

I like to say "the true measure of Christian is to Love those who don't love you." If we can do this, we can say we've arrived. I don't think I am any where close.

Praying for them is the best place to start. Without this step from verse 44 it is not going to happen. Love doesn't come by accident. To love those who aren't crazy about you, is not a natural thing. It takes Prayer, the Word of God, and Patience; Then a little more prayer.

The Fruit of Spirit is only applicable when we show it during less than pleasant circumstances.

Like verse 46 says, even those who don't know Christ can do this much. So to be showing good fruit, that truly tells the world that we are different, it needs to be toward those who don't give a rip about us.

When we can love and forgive the ones who want us destroyed, and then we are like Christ. After being beaten for hours, spit on, lied about, and rejected, Jesus hung on a cross for all of our sins. He used one of his last humanly breaths to forgive the very ones who were in the process of mocking him. That's right, even as they mocked him, he forgave.

Even when we were worthless and have no reason to be forgiven, Jesus reaches out to us and gave us his Grace and Righteousness. He declares us not guilty.

Are or were we any better than those who you can't seem to get along with? Not really. They probably just need to have Jesus and his grace. Until that happens, you need to show the other Fruit; Patience. Do not let them under your skin. It doesn't mean you have to hang out with them, unless the Holy Spirit is telling you to. Just show kindness and gentleness to them, when you are around them.

Remember this will probably take a lot of prayer.

Prayer is good for you.

Day 19

Matthew 6:1- 4 - Praise Seekers

WATCH OUT!

Verse 1 of Chapter 6 starts with a warning.

These four verses are all about bragging. Doing things simply to bring glory to you is pride building. Doing things for the praise is selfishness.

I do this all the time. If you don't give me praise for my good deeds right away, I'll fish for it. For those of you that know me know this is true. I hope that I do things without praise. Not that there is a score card, that I am trying to mark. I feel like I truly love to help people, but I can't say that I do it for the Lord.

I believe this is something I need to work on. Even when I don't fish for the praise, I look for it in silence.

I use to be a lot better at doing things without being noticed. Pick up some trash in the parking lot, pushing the shopping cart all the way back to the collection cage. I do know the rewards for most of the good things I have done, are repaid here on earth. The praise I have received is enough for now.

The true reason to do well is to show the love of Jesus. If we do it for ourselves, we do not bring honor to Jesus. We only bring it to ourselves. Humility is the only thing that gives honor to Jesus.

Humility is not an accident and it is not natural.

Humility comes from Practice, Reading the Word, and Praying specifically for help to be humble.

Lord, help me I need help in a bad way.

I want you to be glorified through me.

DAY 20

Matthew 6: 5 -8 - Prayer part 1

Jesus begins to tell us how to prayer. The Word of God is vital to our relationship. But just as important is our prayer life. Prayer is talking to God. We need to be taught how too. Too many of the religious leaders didn't have a relationship with God so they did not pray correctly. The relationship is important. Without it we don't talk to him like he wishes. He doesn't want us to treat him like a fast food joint. Here's what I want and then just sit waiting, with an attitude, for the order. Oh, and if there is any delay, we get.... well you know how we can get.

SO they didn't know how and when they did pray, because there wasn't a relationship, they didn't pray in private one on one as we would talk to a friend. They only did it as a show.

Do we go down to the altar, at church, for prayer not for an encounter with God, but because others have gone?

Do not just say words that you found in a book, or a prayer that someone e-mailed to you, with a promise to give you good luck.
We must pray to God with an expectation that good things will happen, and this is proper. We should never pray just to get things. The Father knows what we need and will give it, he will even give us more than we ask, if we have the relationship.

Talk to him like a friend. But treat him like a grandfather, showing him the respect he deserves.

Day 21

Matthew 6:9 - Prayer part 2; Pray This Way.

9 Pray like this:
Our Father in heaven, may your name be kept holy.
10 May your Kingdom come soon. May your will be done on earth, as it is in heaven.
11 Give us today the food we need,
12 and forgive us our sins, as we have forgiven those who sin against us.
13 And don't let us yield to temptation, but rescue us from the evil one. NLT

The Lord's Prayer.
Now this is the New Living Translation version, so it is not going to read like you memorized it as a kid, but it is the same prayer.

This is just after Jesus tells us not to use repetitious prayer. Now 2000 years later, many only pray by using the Lord's Prayer word for word. The Lord's Prayer along with the food Prayer, "Come lord Jesus be our guest," has become the only two prayers we utter. I stopped praying the dinner prayer, and now my ad lib prayers have become repetitive.

I am not here to say don't do it, but I don't think he meant for us to us it word for word. But it is the best model. If you mean every word you say and it is spoken with faith, then the repetitive prayers are as good as any others. The danger is in the risk of it becoming a ritual and done without thought or faith.

Faith is the key to **any** and **every** prayer we pray. Faith is what makes prayer work. God is doing the work, but it is the faith that connects it to the worker.

Start with giving God the praise and acknowledge his Lordship.

Pray that God's will, will be done here on earth and in your own life, including work, family, ministry, etc.

Pray for the Lord's return.
Pray for the needs we have; food, work, love, protection on the home, family.

Don't stop before asking for forgiveness and the help we need to forgive others.

Forgiving others is also very important for us and the kingdom of God.

Lastly, please Lord, help us get through another day, and avoid the things that tempt us.
Protect us from our true enemies, the demons and the devil.

When you pray please pray with humility, with love, and pray as if you are talking to your grandfather.

We get so easily caught up in our needs, which is part of it, but a very small percentage of it. Jesus is here reminding us to keep on the big picture; God's will and praying for others.

When we pray we should have these five elements:

Give God Praise,
Pray for God's will.
Pray for help and needs.
Pray for forgiveness.
Pray that we'll stay strong.

Don't pray one dimensionally. Pray the 5 point prayer. I guess it would form a star if we drew it out.

Day 22

Matthew 6:14 & 15 – Forgiving Others

14 "If you forgive those who sin against you, your heavenly Father will forgive you.
15 But if you refuse to forgive others, your Father will not forgive your sins. NLT

This is the most dangerous verse in the whole Bible.

Verse 14 starts off OK. This is great if we can forgive then God will forgive us. That's easy. Well may be not easy, but no threat. I will try my best, and forgive everyone I can. I'll do my best. I will work on Forgiving and be just fine.
Just Fine; Right?

If I could skip Verse 15 that is. It's this part about 'God not forgive?', that is going to be a problem. Wait a minute. What about Grace and Love? How can this be? I'm not sure if I can forgive everyone. I can? What if I don't want to?

My Salvation depends upon it. I've got to.

Here it is. God won't give grace to any one who does not give grace. This of course is after we get saved. Once we accept his grace, then we need to share the grace with others.

If we choose not to give grace to others, we are left with unclaimed sin. This is sin that we choose not to repent of. If we do not repent of it, then it is not washed away. Sin cannot go to heaven. Unless Jesus wipes out the sin it is still there.

Step 1: Admit the un-forgiveness is a sin and repent.
Step 2: pray for help. We can't forgive without the help of the Holy Spirit. Call on his help. Forgiving others is not always easy; it's ok to get help. In fact, it's the only way.

Verse 15 cannot be ignored, but it can be possible with God's help.

Forgiving others makes us healthier Christians and draws us closer to God than ever before. Not only or salvation, but our relationship depends on it. Forgiveness will give you peace. Peace that only comes for the Holy Spirit. Unforgiveness can also hinder others from finding forgiveness in Jesus. So it not only hurt ourselves, it also hurts others.

Verse 15 is all about the Holy Spirit. Without him we can't do it. I we chose not to forgive, then we turn our back on him and this is Blasphemy.

The sin is in the ignoring the Holy Spirit, who prompts us to forgive. It is called Blasphemy.

Matt 12:31 "So I tell you, every sin and blasphemy can be forgiven--except blasphemy against the Holy Spirit, which will never be forgiven." NLT

Let the Grace work through you and share it with some one you hate. Making the Hate go away.

Day 23

Matthew 6:16&18 - Fasting

Fasting?

Jesus instructs us how to do it, so it must be important. At this point in his sermon, he is still pointing out all the things that tradition and habits have lead the people to doing wrong. Here once again it is pride that starts off the topic.

Fasting is to be a vow between you and God. The minute we draw attention to the fact we are sacrificing for the Lord, the fast might as well be over. We break the vow, by drawing attention to ourselves, instead of God. In our vow we need to focus on God. The fast is to draw us closer to God. When we start to brag about our fast, we draw closer to the world. The opposite happens.

Fasting can be from just about anything. There are some who are very strict on how a fast should be done. Fasting is traditionally abstaining from food or drink. A 40 day fast is food free during the day time; many believe a Jewish Fast was until sun down. It may be from all food or just some foods. It may be from a specific drink. In my opinion fasting from something can be just about anything. I think it should be from something that would be difficult to stay away from. There is a group of kids I know that are praying for the lost in Memphis. They are fasting Facebook, Video Games, and TV. Now for a Teen these are hard things.
My wife fasts Diet Coke.

As we get the craving for the things we have set aside, that's when we pray. That is when we think about the thing we are lifting up to the Lord.

Food is the best, because there is no way to ignore or forget about what you've given up.

If you fast for one day from all food, it will be about 9 am and food will be all you think about. As often as you would think about food, should be the frequency in your prayers. By noon, it would be a constant reminder of the Cause and Jesus. By Dinner time, you are praying like never before, and your stomach is praying along with you with groans.

Plenty of Water and day two, your prayers are at a whole new level as you doubt if you can actually make to the end of the day. You are now reading the Bible every chance you get for help to make it through.

In the case of the kids; the time that they would normally spend doing an activity would be spent in prayer and bible study. Setting time aside for Jesus is tough. A fast can help stay focused and keep you in tune and focused on Jesus.

A fast is not skipping lunch because you forgot your money. It is a vow to the Lord as you pray for a need or situation. Don't brag about it.

Turning our cravings and our weaknesses into prayers, is a great way to build up you relationship with the Lord.

Fasting is not meant to be a way to hurt yourself to prove your dedication to God. God does not want us to hurt ourselves or anyone else to prove anything. The only way to prove our dedication to the Lord is to love others and to obey him.

Day 24

Matthew 6: 19-21 & 24 – Money and Joy

Verse 19 thru 24 is all about Money verses the Lord.

    God wants us to prosper. He wants us to be happy. He knows that money does not bring Joy. Joy is much better than happiness. Happiness is dependant on circumstances, while joy is not. Joy can sustain you even in hard times. Happiness comes from temporary things. Joy comes from the Lord. But everything needs to be in balance.

    We can get caught up on buying things, which can bring happiness. I love trips to Wal-Mart and Costco. But some of us buy things just to have things. "I've got to complete my collection." "I don't have the blue one." "This will look great with my new shoes." We have plenty of excuses. Someone may spend $10,000 for a boat that will put us on the same level as the guys at work. Now it sits week after week in the drive way, only to be taken out once a year. Waste of money? The motivation behind each purchase it is the real test. Why did you buy it? Was the Lord leading you to give some money to a ministry or a person in need? If we spend our money as fast as we get it, we are not able to bless others with it, and can miss out on some major blessings ourselves. Storing our treasures in heaven means we are sharing our money. We don't have to give it all away, but we should be generous.

    Storing up our treasures in our garage or attic is not benefiting anyone.

    We can't serve two. If we are selfish in our lives, and serve only ourselves with our money, it shows where our heart is. But if we give freely and willingly, as the Holy Spirit leads.

    Tithe is not an option. It is a law. 10% of what we make goes to the store house (local church). Our offerings and extra giving is above this. Your money can bring happiness to others and lead to Joy for yourself.

    Joy is forever.

Day 25

Matthew 6; 25 - 34 - Don't worry.

If you haven't been, you really need to pull out your bible and read these verses for yourself.

The main thing Jesus is pointing out is "Don't Worry."

It was a simpler time, in some ways, except lack of running water. We have added a lot more things to worry about today, but the main worries haven't changed; work, money, and providing for the family. Job Losses still happen. Bad weeks still happen. Things that we can't control happen all the time. So what hasn't changed? The fact we have little control over most of the things in our lives.

Verse 27; *"Can it add a single day to life?"* NLT. This is a great reminder of why it's pointless to worry. There is nothing to gain by worrying. Worry is in fact the opposite of faith. So when we worry, and that's all that we think about, we are giving up on God's ability to help us. Even worse we don't think he will help us.

Verse 33: The righteousness of Jesus is first, and then we need to choose to live in his grace. Once this is done, Jesus will give us everything we need. We also need to give to God. Tithe is important to the promise. We need to stay righteous, by staying humble and giving to God.

Verse 34; tomorrow is never as bad as we dreamed it would be, in our dream or worries. Thinking about tomorrow and worrying about how we are going to survive, or what the boss will do to us. Worry about friends giving up on us.

Worry, just DON'T do it.

Verse 32; God already knows, so there is no reason to worry. If we think about worries to the point where we are self absorbed, we stop thinking about God or others.

We need to think about good stuff. And praise God.

Day 26

Matthew 7:1 – Judge Not

Jesus keeps hitting us below the belt. If there was a prize for judging others, I'd have a trophy case full. Here Jesus is telling us to not do something many of us have gotten so good at.

I can't say it isn't a fair rule to go by. How can we ask God to judge us with Mercy, if we don't show a little mercy ourselves. Again this is not a rule to those who are looking for a first time relationship with Jesus. He is talking to the people of faith in Israel. He is talking about us, the Christians of today. We have been saved by grace. Grace is now the very thing we need to share.

When we judge and come up with reasons that others can't get to heaven, or just shouldn't be at church, we are not sharing grace or mercy.

We don't want others to judge us and limit us in any way. So why is it we do it to others so easily.

We better not limit others by our own judgment.

We are God's mouth piece. If we cast judgment on someone, how are they going to know that Jesus will forgive them? How will they know? How will they change? How will they ever know Grace?

I see it like this. We have the power to share the grace, or to keep it from others. If we keep it from others I do believe it is worse than a sin we do on our own.

I pray that I am never the reason that someone else misses out on Heaven.

Jesus should be the one we point everyone to. Even the ones we don't think deserve it. After all we never deserved it either.

Day 27

Matthew 7:3-5 – Don't Judge People

3 "And why worry about a speck in your friend's eye when you have a log in your own?
4 How can you think of saying to your friend, 'Let me help you get rid of that speck in your eye,' when you can't see past the log in your own eye?
5 Hypocrite! First get rid of the log in your own eye; then you will see well enough to deal with the speck in your friend's eye.
NLT

This is something I don't have as big of a problem as I once did. It took a few years to realize, there is more than one way of doing things. Even though someone else isn't doing it the way I would, it doesn't mean they are doing it wrong. Many are quick to condemn when someone doesn't fulfill all the requirements that they think the individual should.

Question 1: Are you responsible for the actions of that person?
Answer: If they do not work for you, and aren't your children, then the answer is NO.

Question 2: Do you really think that you could do it better?
Answer: Better means that you would not only cover the parts that you see as a failure, but also every other aspect. This means, even the ones that went flawlessly. No one is perfect. If you got one aspect perfect, there is probably another area that would be weak. This only leaves areas for someone else to complain about, you.

Question 3: Are you so narrow minded, that you can only see the flaws of an event or situation.
Answer: That's what Jesus meant in verse 5, about being a hypocrite.

To hold someone up to a standard that we ourselves can't live up to, makes us a hypocrite. This falls right into the same category as withholding grace from those of our choosing.

Matthew – Jesus Speaks

A friend of mine gets grief about not being in full control all the time. Should we make him something he is not? No! He is not a policeman. He's not a law enforcer. If that's all we look at then we are in great error. Truth: He loves like most of us only hope to. He has a gentleness about him that is probably closer to Jesus than I have ever been. So if he is guilty of being too much like Jesus, then how is that a bad thing?

Please do not cast judgment around, like you could do it better. If God has called you to take over, then do it without complaint. If he hasn't called you to do it, then the only option unless actual harm is at risk, is to pray. Complaining doesn't help anyone, no matter how much you think it does.

I do say you can seek council with a Pastor or elder, if you are open to the truth, and not just looking for someone to agree with you. Talking it through is good, when done in the right way.
If we simply are looking for someone to agree, then that is not the right way.

Sorry for the harshness. This has hurt many of my friends, and causes division in the church. So I am bias. I hate it. Doesn't mean I don't do it. I am guilty. I need to try even harder and be more careful.

Day 28

Matthew 7:7&8 – Asking and Waiting

7 "Keep on asking, and you will receive what you ask for. Keep on seeking, and you will find. Keep on knocking, and the door will be opened to you.
8 For everyone who asks, receives. Everyone who seeks, finds. And to everyone who knocks, the door will be opened. NLT

Verse 7 tells us to keep on asking. I don't think we can ask too much.

Is it possible to get on the Lord's nerves? I don't think so. He's probably not much more of a fan of whinny than any of us. I'm not talking about whinny. I'm talking about heart felt humble prayers. Even pleading in desperation is sweet to his ears. When we ask, we display our faith.

When I say ask, I mean out load. When we pray it has to be out loud. Prayers in our head, is simply meditation. Which in itself is not bad, but to display your faith we need to pray. To get the result Jesus is promising here in verse 8, we need to be vocal about it.

Say it so not just heaven hears, but also so the devil and his demons hear.

I can't tell you for sure why God makes us wait. But I made a list of reasons that it may be. You won't know which reason is yours until after you receive the answer. Just remember the answer will come, even if it takes a while.

1. Other people God will use to give the best answer aren't ready yet.
2. The situation has not reached the prime point. God has a few more things to put in place first.
3. Perhaps you aren't ready yet. We can grow a bunch in the period of waiting, as we seek after God. We can actually get closer to God in our prayer time and in the time of waiting. (I know some of you know this first hand. praying for a loved one, who is sick. Knowing you can't do anything, so you call on God, in your desperation you call on God as never before,

and you found your faith building even before the answer came.)
4. The perfect answer takes perfect timing, and that time hasn't come yet.
5. There is a break through that has to happen first and you are very close.
6. There is a new level of growth God has in store for you, and you are half way there.
7. You have something special to learn.
8. Someone else needs to see you and hear your testimony. Your testimony is not complete, until all the pieces are in place.

Never give up on prayer.

Never give up on God.

Look every day to see what the Holy Spirit is doing, sometimes you can see it if you look.

Read your bible to build your faith. (Faith comes by hearing, hearing the word of God.)

Day 29

Matthew 7:9 – 11 - Good gifts

Jesus wants what it best for us. He knows what is best for us better than we do. So sometimes it is a little different than we think we need or want. His timing isn't the same as ours as I have pointed out before.

The Faith we need to have for his love and grace to shower blessings on us needs to be on his goodness. We need to have faith that he wants only what is good for us.

When things are good, it's a given that God is good. However, when things are dragging you down and the answers aren't coming, it is easy to doubt. Questions about whether or not God wants you to be happy or whether he wants what we want. We even question if he even cares or whether we are being punished.

REMEMBER: God is on your side.

The best result will come if you stay faithful. This means you don't complain, and display your dis-belief. Grumbling will result in missed blessings.

We also need to stay in prayer. Stay in Jesus and keep on asking. I'm not talking about selfish prayers. You know what a selfish request is, so I don't have to explain that. The Holy Spirit will let you know if you are on target, if you pray and listen.

Prayer needs to be accompanied by quiet time and a chance to hear from God. Hearing from God can also come from reading your Bible.

God is good, he want to be good to you, if you let him.

The gifts that he has for you are good. Stay faithful and have patients, the gifts that you wait for are better. When they are from God they are good and perfect.

Day 30

Matthew 7:12 - Do Unto Others

12 "Do to others whatever you would like them to do to you. This is the essence of all that is taught in the law and the prophets. NLT

Verse 12 is also known as the GOLDEN RULE. If you follow it, you will have a better chance to have friends. You will be more likely to be respected. You will be following God's law to a T.

If you follow it, Commandments 4 thru 10 are covered.

I find myself at a point where, there isn't much to add.
It just needs to be put out there as a reminder.

I would have to say this includes complaining about people and the things they do.

Bottom line, BE NICE. That's an order.

Even though I really don't feel like being nice all the time. Following Jesus isn't about feelings though. It is about following, regardless of how we feel.

DAY 31

Matthew 7:15-20 - Watch who you follow

Verse 15; Beware!
 I don't really have to say a whole lot on this subject, other than read the word. The word is where we get our wisdom, and insight. When we are studied up and full of his word, we can see clearly the false teachings. This does not mean you have several chapters memorized, or be a scholar. You just need to keep it fresh in your mind. The Holy Spirit can lead you to the right verse on the day you need it. He can't do this if you aren't reading it. SO just read it.

Verse 16; we know when someone is all talk. Too much talk is often a cover up of the lack of fruit. Is there love in what they say? Is there love in the way they say it? Is their motive to lift Jesus up or to lift themselves up, as they pretend to lift up Jesus?

 Good fruit is sweet and maybe a bit tart. Good fruit is not overly bitter or harmful.

Fruits: Love, Gentleness, Peaceful, Kind.

 So beware. Watch out for and limit your time with them. Avoid them. Stay away. Their bad fruit even if it is covered in a caramel coating, will still be unhealthy. Not just unhealthy, but bad for you. Don't listen to it.

 I will say it takes staying in the word, because most of the time they may be very well liked by many, and what they say won't be clearly seen as wrong at first look. Just like the devil in the garden, he tricked them by slightly twisting what God had told them. When the Early Christians were trying to reinstitute the total law and hold gentiles to it, they were mostly right, until they insinuated or told them out right that they could be saved without certain rules. They were wrong and corrected by Paul and Peter.

Day 32

Matthew 7:21 – Not Everyone Will

We just finished looking at knowing people by their fruit. Now we see part two. Not only have we been warned to stay away from them, Jesus is saying they are not part of his family.

The Holy Spirit told me the other night, that I cannot judge my relationship on whether or not God is using me. God will use people even if they do not follow him. He uses who he chooses to, to meet the needs as he sees fit. Nehemiah needed help from a pagan king; God used the king to allow them safe passage to Judah, and money to re-build. God used Pilot to condemn Jesus and declare him not guilty. Jonah was used to bring a message of hope and salvation to Nineveh. Jonah had given up on Jesus, but God still used him.

So if I share a good message or God gives me the right words to say, it doesn't mean I am in God's perfect will. It is possible that God would still use me to help others, despite myself.

What matters is my relationship with Jesus, Repentance, and Service.

Most of the laws and promises are a rule that works for both Christians and non-Christians, which is what Jonah had a problem with. If a Non-Christian shows love they will reap love. Sowing money and sharing with the poor, will result in blessings. This cannot be mistaken for a perfect walk with Jesus.

So what's my point?

Relationship and repentance are more important than signs and wonders. As we tap into the Holy Spirit and our relationship grows deeper, we can be used for even bigger miracles.

Not everyone who thinks they are safe is. If you have the forgiveness, and you know you can't live without Jesus, you're probably OK.

Day 33

Matthew 7:24-27 - Built on Jesus

Life is a whirlwind. The storms of life just keep coming. I think this is the pattern we are all facing until the glorious day, when Jesus takes us home to Heaven.
Jesus sometimes protects us from the on-slot, if not he always helps us bare it.

Verse 24; Jesus is telling us how to endure. If we listen to his teaching, we will be wise and be solid as a rock.
Today we don't have a mountain to go to and listen to Jesus live. We do have the Bible. In a way it is better. I can keep a copy in my car, at my desk, or in my room. I can even look it up online. If Jesus was still here, the chances of him being in my car to tell me stories, is pretty slim. But I can read his words any time I want. The more I read the wiser I get. The wiser I get the stronger I get. I feel weak more times than I care to mention. But I have weathered a bunch of storms. I have seen Jesus help me through and my faith is stronger than ever. And each storm brings more faith and more wisdom.

If we read his word and reject or say in our mind it isn't true, then we are fools and Jesus can't help. We will be all alone when the storms hit. There for like a house on sand.

When I lived in Virginia Beach I saw the effects of beach houses after a storm. The houses start on stilts. When you walk by and the living room is now in the sand and you can walk right in without the need for a door, it's a bad day.

When the bad day comes don't be left with your rooms falling off into the sand and waves. Let Jesus be at your side. Read the word regularly before the storm. Believe what it says and live it. Then Jesus will help you make it through. Enjoy the times when Jesus blocks the storm completely. He is still in the Miracle business.

Believe it.

Day 34

Matthew 8:3-4 - He is Willing

3 Jesus reached out and touched him. "I am willing," he said. "Be healed!" And instantly the leprosy disappeared.
4 Then Jesus said to him, "Don't tell anyone about this. Instead, go to the priest and let him examine you. Take along the offering required in the law of Moses for those who have been healed of leprosy. This will be a public testimony that you have been cleansed." NLT

    Verse 3 is a very important part of Faith.
The first step in a Miracle is believing in Jesus and who he is.
The second step is believing he can do the miracle.
The third step is the key to verse 3. We need to believe Jesus is **willing** to do the miracle.

    I say that verse 3 is where we find that Jesus is willing. The doubt of this keeps us from asking. Or at best we go and have someone else pray for us, but don't really believe that anything will happen. We need to believe that he will do it and then ask with the assurance that he is capable of doing it.
    Pray also for God's will to be done, and just trust him.

    Verse 4 shows Jesus' desire for the testimony of this man to be verified, before he starts to share it. He told him to follow the law and go to be checked out by the priest. (There weren't doctors) Then let the testimony not just come from his own lips but from the priest.

    When we see the miracles happening in our own life, let others verify it for you. Then you can tell others about what the Lord has done, and others can be lifted up by your miracle and maybe even believe in a miracle for themselves.

    So today as you find or make time for prayer. **Believe!** For Jesus is willing.

    His love has no end for you.

Day 35

Matthew 8:7 - Pray for Others

Verse 7 finds Jesus responding to a Roman soldier who is asking for help. Not for himself, but for a servant. Jesus responds even before the soldier had a chance to finish talking or even before he actually asked for help.

I get several things from these six words.

First is the willingness of Jesus to go. As soon as he heard the need and saw the faith of the soldier, he was ready to go.

Second is that Jesus was responding before he asked. This may not seem fair, if you have been asking and it doesn't seem like Jesus is responding. The response is not in the asking, it's in his faith as we will see farther into the scripture.

His faith was great. But that's still not the whole story.

Thirdly; the soldier didn't just go to God Begging for help. He started talking to him. He just started a conversation about the needs of his servant. Jesus wants to hear from us. Not just with whining, and demands, but an actual conversation.

Fourthly; this is the first scripture we have looked at that shows someone praying for someone else. The soldier is lifting up the needs of others. This is done without the servant showing any faith. Jesus hasn't actually made contact with the servant and still he heals the servant.

Talk to Jesus he wants to hear from you. He wants to have a conversation with you.

Pray for others and have faith that Jesus will respond. Then look for the miracles to start.

Day 36

Matthew 8:26 – Faith in the Storm

26 Jesus responded, "Why are you afraid? You have so little faith!" Then he got up and rebuked the wind and waves, and suddenly there was a great calm. NLT

Verse 26 is in the midst of a storm. The disciples were scared and fighting for their lives. Peter, John, James, and Andrew were all fishermen. They knew the sea. They knew the capability of the boat. I guess that those 4 were not nearly as scared as the ones who may have been new to water travel.

When in the midst of the storm, they were only thinking about themselves, their own survival. They were not thinking about the savior in their midst. They didn't stop to think through Jesus' purpose. If he was on earth to save it and he was sent by God. How could any thing happen to him? How can he fulfill his purpose from under the sea?

When the disciplines finally thought about Jesus;
They didn't look to him as a savior.
They didn't look to him for a miracle.
They simply looked at him as a man.

In fact they looked at him as a man that wasn't pulling his weight. He wasn't bailing water or working the crash crew. He was just laying there in the boat sleeping.

Jesus is woken up. Not to help with the work, but to tell them the truth. "You guys have no faith!"

If they had went to Jesus and asked for help, just as we do when we pray, the reaction would have been different. I don't believe their lack of faith was from waking him up. I believe it was by them looking at him as a man, with a limited means to help. He wasn't at that time the Son of God. He was a no load, as we use to say in the Navy.

Our lack of faith starts with us forgetting that Jesus is in control and can calm our storm.

Today's lesson on FAITH:

We need to believe that Jesus is the Son of God and can do anything. Nothing is out of his control.

Believe nothing is a surprise to Him. He wants what's best for you and wants you to have a blessed life.

Believe before you see the proof and Jesus' love reveled.

Don't doubt Jesus' love and his ability during the storm you are going through.

Day 37

Matthew 9:2 – Be Encouraged

Don't worry today.
Don't worry tomorrow.

If you were brought to the Lord by a friend or any other means, be encouraged.
If you look to Jesus you will be forgiven.
If you ask it will be given.

In this case we find a man who was paralyzed, and could do nothing on his own. In this case Jesus gave him the gift of healing. But either way, the fact is, even if he didn't get up and walk, he would have been forgiven. Forgiveness is worth much more than a healing. It is eternal.
A healing is limited to the next sickness, or death.
I do believe that Jesus heals still today. So this is not to discourage a request for healing.
Healings come and sometimes they don't.
But Forgiveness comes every time;
Every time we humbly ask for forgiveness.

Be encouraged, Jesus is here for you. What is it you need? Go to him. Ask someone to help you get to him.

If you need me, call me. I'll be glad to help.

Day 38

Matthew 9:5&6 – Forgiveness: The key to Healing.

Verse 5 is Jesus' response to the leaders in the church's reaction. They had condemned Jesus for saying he could forgive sin. They we not ready to begin or even begin to believe Jesus was really God's son. If someone who was not God's son, made the claims he is making, then they would be lying and it would be blasphemy.

Jesus wasn't just talk. He proved himself over and over again. Here in verse 6 he sets the challenge. "I'm going to prove that I have the power." He turned to the crippled man and said get up and walk.

We all know what happened next.

See Jesus isn't a mad man that is making crazy claims. He wasn't standing at the airport with a sign, claiming the end is near.
He let the actions talk for themselves.

How is there a correlation between Sin and Healing?

Remember things were perfect in the Garden of Eden. Before the fall, man knew no sickness, birth defects, or trauma. All this was added to man with the fall of man. When Adam took that bite and then lied about it. From then on sickness and death has been in the world.

It is sin that corrupts our body and even the earth itself. Healing comes from the effects of sin being removed. They can't be removed without forgiveness.
Forgiveness is the key to ALL healing.

The greatest of all healing, is the healing of the soul and the forgiveness of sin, which brings eternal life. Not eternal life in the current body, unless the Lord comes back soon.

Be healed today. Call on Jesus. Ask first for forgiveness.

Day 39

Matthew 9:12 – Help takes Sacrifice

It is really easy for me to want to help people that are friendly and nice. Sometimes I try to help people that don't need help at all. I imagine this more annoying than anything else. Helping people who don't need help is actually very easy. Since, they don't need the help, so the amount you give can be limited, by your own comfort level. You can back out at any time and no one gets hurt.

To help someone that really needs help. This is hard. Once you start, when can you stop? In some cases, you may never stop. It will most likely be well past any comfort level. To help people that really need help and are in bad shape, takes sacrifice.

Sacrifice is giving something that has a high cost, monetarily, time, or emotion. So to help people that are hurting, will take sacrifice. But the rewards are un-measurable.

Jesus in verse 12 was talking to those who wanted Jesus to give them all his attention. They didn't even realize they need him on an eternal level. They only want Jesus to be their friend because of how popular he was. If he was a prophet, they want to be on his side. To waste his greatness on the sick, poor, and unwanted, was just ridiculous, in their minds. It is this mind set that caused them to despise Jesus.

To Jesus' point; they were having no troubles in life. Since his time here on earth was short, his time would be better spent on the sick.

Jesus knew those who were on the edge. No hope at all. The people with no hope at all are Jesus' specialty. He is close to the broken hearted and wants to help.

If you are going through a rough time, call on Jesus, he wants to help you.

Day 40

Matthew 9:13 - Knowing your need

Here's a look at God's Law verses Love. Here's the reason this is so hard for so many. There is control in the Law. The law is something we can claim as well as claim victory.

The Law is not alone. It can also be tradition, grabbing hold of traditions that are easy to keep and make us feel better about the life we are leading.

Love is hard. There is no control in love. When we love, we cannot control if the love is returned. We cannot control other's reaction. We can't control who and how others love. We can't even control who we love sometimes. There are going to be more times than we care to mention, that we will show love to people that don't care. The chance of this increases, as we reach out to the whole world and not just those who love us.

As verse 13 says, we must learn the meaning of the scriptures. Show mercy; when the laws and traditions tell us to kill, or separate.

Jesus did not come for those who won't admit they need him. He did come to save those who know they are sinners and are lost. When any of us get to the point when we realize we can't make it without Jesus. This is when we can move forward to salvation and a relationship with Jesus.

See if we are bound by tradition or the law, we aren't held back by anything from God. It is our own insecurity, that holds us back, along with our own denials and search for self worth. If we search for ways that are easy and won't make us uncomfortable, we end up remaining uncomfortable in our own way, and still lost.

When we realize that we need him and see the hope in Jesus for the asking, we can ask and find the truth that Jesus loves even the most messed up people. So it doesn't matter who we are or what we've done. All it takes is repentance and admitting that we need Jesus, then our sins (even the worst of them) are washed away.

Day 41

Matthew 9:22 – Faith Opens the Eyes

Verse 22 we find a repeat of the healing after Jesus tells them to "Be encouraged."

Be encouraged help is on the way.

Jesus is on the way.

It is always the Faith that brings the healing and the encouragement and the answer and the miracle.

SO let us have faith.
Faith comes from the Word of God. The Bible.

If you want the faith to be encouraged, read the bible.
If you want the faith to be healed, read the word.
If you want to know Jesus, read the word.

Verse 22 is the end of the story of the women that touched his hem. She had the faith to fight the crowd. Faith that not only can Jesus heal her, but faith for even more. She believed that all she had to do, was touch him. His anointing was that strong. She saw it in Jesus, while most of the crowd did not. Even some of the 12 disciples were still struggling with this fact.

She saw it because she had faith. Lack of faith causes spiritual blindness.

Open your eyes, read God's word.

Spiritual Blindness is a bad thing. It causes loneliness and depression.

Don't be depressed, read the Bible.

Day 42

Matthew 9:28 – Vocalize Your Faith

As we will see through out the ministry of Jesus, it is common for Jesus to ask questions he already knows the answer to. Verse 28 is no different. He asks the question, not to find out the answer, but to hear the answer.

Vocalizing our faith is extremely important. Today we aren't going to hear Jesus ask us audibly. But we can still vocalize our faith, in prayer. Remember Prayer isn't prayer unless it is out loud. We can also vocalize our faith when we ask others to pray with us and tell them about how you believe in Jesus. For example, "I know Jesus can heal me, will you please join me in prayer."

Vocalize it when you talk about a situation you have been praying for, by saying only positive things. Complaining does not show faith. It actually shows lack of faith, and vocalizes disbelief.

We will see also, how Jesus has people do things to show their faith. Putting your faith into action is equally important, if that is what the Holy Spirit is telling you to do.

Today we will stick with vocalizing it. You can start by vocalizing through e-mail and send me a message. Tell me what you are praying and believing for. You can also tell someone that has faith. I would say only tell other believers. And then only tell believers with real faith. Avoid those who are prone to complaining, and doubtful talk. They can drag you down, and make you question your faith. But find that person, who will pray with you and encourage you.

We need to encourage others, and be around those who encourage us. This does not mean we do not reach out to the lost; it is strictly for confiding in with needs and prayer requests.

I wish Jesus was the only thing I vocalize. So do the others I work with.

Day 43

Matthew 9:37 & 38 – Be a Worker

If you have ever served in a church, you know that this is still true today. Every time there is a special event at the church, it's the same group of people that are working it. I am blessed to be in a church that has a higher percentage of volunteers than most. There is however too many people that do not help. This makes verse 37 still true today.

Another way the few are working alone is in the tithe. Tithe is a command from God for us to give 10% of our earnings to the local church. It's better than taxes. We get to pick the local church. So we can make sure it is going to a church that is vibrant and reaching out to poor and elderly.

It is rare for a church to have even 50% of the congregation tithing. If they did can you imagine how many more people we could reach? For Raleigh, we could build a half way house, give even more food and cloths to the poor. Build a better building to serve the community even more effectively. The possibilities are endless.

Jesus tells us to pray for more workers. SO we need to pray. We need to continue to ask friends and new people to help. Sometimes it's just a matter of letting them know you need them, and that they are welcome to serve with you.

If you aren't helping, it's not too late. Jesus has a harvest ready just for you. Go out and bring it in. This can be through the church or maybe start a book club, bible study, or prayer time for you and your neighbors. You could even do it at or before work.

People Need Jesus. You can be the one to show them Jesus.

Day 44

Matthew 10:8 – Giving Back

Jesus is giving instructions for the disciples on one of their walk about, to heal, cast out demons, and bless people. Jesus gave a lot of instructions that are just for them, praying for the sick and the other things that happened when they prayed wasn't. These instructions are given to more of us after the Holy Spirit came.

Verse 8 had one part that is still good for us all to follow, "give freely." We have had so much given to us; we need to give back to the world just as God has given to us.

What can we give?

Money, food, or stuff that clutters our house.

Forgiveness? Jesus has forgiven us for so much more than anyone could have done to us.

Kindness; it isn't always easy, but it can be worth more than money.

Gentleness; in our selfishness and our rush of our own lives, we can be harsh. Not always on purpose, but harsh just the same.

Help; holding a door, giving a helping hand to a neighbor, and more.

Look for ways you can help, or ways you can give. Jesus has given us life itself, eternal life on top of that. We give back to him by giving to others.

Day 45

Matthew 10:24 & 25 – Don't Give Up

Verse 24 is referencing the place of a slave or student. This is not a reference between us and our slave driving bosses. What Jesus is talking about is, our relation with him. No matter how good we get, we will never be better than him. Jesus will never be our servant. We need to never forget where our place is.

He is the Lord of the entire universe. We are weak at best, but the lie that we sometimes listen to, is we are some how able to be more. Ask Adam and Eve how that worked out for them. It hasn't stopped there. The Church of Scientology is all about this lie. So we need to keep our perspective.

He is preparing the disciples for their journey. They are about to go out on their own and do what Jesus has been doing; Healing, Demon stopping, and other Miracles. Even though Jesus shared perfect love and was the most gentle and kind person that ever walked the earth, he always knew what to say and what to do, yet he had as many enemies as he had friends.

He was telling them to not get too stuck on their new abilities, that no matter how good they are to those around them, they will not be loved by everyone. We can cause our selves self condemnation, because someone doesn't like what we do, even when we do good things.

Rejection is hard; very hard. But it will happen. This does not mean you are a bad person. For even the best of us have enemies. It doesn't mean we should give up. It means we are more like Christ than we may have thought. Even as our savior was rejected, we will be rejected in some manner. When we are, we need to not let it stop us. We need to shake the dust off our feet and move on and continue to do well. Continue to do what God has called you to do. Never give up. Remember Jesus kept going even to the cross. Even as he was hanging on the cross, he didn't stop. He turned and forgave the retentive thief.

Day 46

Matthew 10:28 – Why Fear, What can They Do?

28 "Don't be afraid of those who want to kill your body; they cannot touch your soul. Fear only God, who can destroy both soul and body in hell. NLT

Verse 28 is a reminder that these bodies we are in are only temporary, so don't get too attached. What is the worst that can happen? Most would say death. But death when we are a child of God only leads to heaven and Jesus face to face. So how can this be the worst? Now torture and living in pain is the worst.

I stay alive to serve God in the way he has planned. I believe he has a work for me to do. I have a family, but it is up to God on how long they are my responsibility. I want to be here for them of course, but it is up to God. If he calls me home, I know he will provide for them. Death is only hard on the ones left behind.

But the point Jesus is making isn't about that. It is about not fearing the world. The world can only harm your temporary home. It can't touch your eternity. No one has the power to do anything to your soul or your eternity. We have the only controls. We can choose to let influences cause us to question our eternity. This is why the Word of God is so important. The Bible builds our faith so we don't listen to the lies. So if we are not to be afraid of death, what else can they do? Should we hold back from serving God, because of what others think? Absolutely not! Fear of others is actually ridiculous, but we can find ourselves in hiding because of this fear.

REMEMBER, they can't take anything away from you that really counts. They can't take away anything Jesus has given you. So don't slowdown and just show others about Jesus.

He is in control. We're just along for the ride. Let us live that ride to the fullest, and experience every thing the Lord has to offer.

Day 47

Matthew 10:29 – The Value of You

Does God find value in you?   YES.

Verse 29 through 31 is about your value. Not just more than a sparrow, but a whole flock.

TRUTH: Jesus finds value in you, so don't feel worthless. Never believe that you are less than perfection in God's eyes. God sees us a lot differently than man. He can see right through us, down to the core. Even though he can see our every fault, even though we can't hide our sin from him, he sees much more than that. God does not see the sins that Jesus has covered by his blood.

So how can God see only the good?   Easy.   Jesus.

When we ask for forgiveness, we are forgiven and those sins are covered.

He sees our future. He sees our true potential. He sees how he can use our talents. He sees how he can use your gifts. He can see how much love you can and will give back to him. He can see how you will share the Love of Jesus with others. He can see you being blessed. He can see you blessing others. He can see how beautiful you truly are, even if you don't see it or feel it yourself.

You are more valuable than the most precious of metals or gems. You are AWESOME in God's eyes.

Be all you can be. Ask Jesus to make you a better you, living up to your true potential.

Day 48

Matthew 10:37 – God's Love

Verse 37 uses the one thing most of us hold very dear, Family. If we love our family this is good. Family is the first place we are able to share love. It is also the first place we can display love in action. It is a great start. But it is an easy way to love in most cases. We always have at least one family member that is a little harder to love than others. But it is easy to love your Mom, even when she isn't a good one. Sharing love outside of the family is not as easy. The second place we share love is the Church. Again this can be easy. We are mostly surrounded by people that encourage us and are fairly easy to love, because they are so nice. (In some cases anyways).

But to love outside these two places is more difficult, like loving those who don't return the love. How about giving acts of kindness and love to those you don't know or even those who are different from us. To share the Love of Jesus as Jesus would have us do, means to share the Love outside family, both blood and church.

Moving on to this point, requires us to first love God. This should be our deepest love. Loving God the savior of our soul.

The fact of Loving God is more than a one way relationship. It is a three way street.

Let me explain.

The closer we get to God, the close we get to the true and ultimate source of love. Our ability to receive love increases as the love is given back to us. (Truthfully God loved us first) Anyways, we now are tapped into the vine of loving life. This love now can flow through us not just into us. As we let the love flow out of us in acts of kindness and love, the ones around us benefit. The love goes out to the ones we love and hopefully the ones that are just brought to us by the Holy Spirit. If you really want to love your wife, kids, and parents the best you can. Love God more. Because the more you love God, and develop that relationship, the better your capacity to love the ones you already love.

Love God first and the love that comes from him will make you a better love sharer.

Day 49

Matthew 10:38 & 39 – Pride

If you were wondering what it means to take up your cross? I'm not going to tell you.

The really meaning behind verse 38 and 39 is;

PRIDE

That's it boiled down to one word.

When we put our desires above our relationship with God, we are loosing. Everything you are trying to hold on to, that you know is holding you back form serving God the way you know you have been called to, is bad. Bad in the sense that it not only holds you back from your top service, but it also holds you back from a better and closer relationship. Ultimately the very thing you hold on to so strongly can become the very thing that separates you from him and separation means no heaven.

So why is it pride? The reason we hold on, in most cases is pride. We don't want to let go of the things that make us feel better, or a sense of security. The pride in thinking the things we hold onto will some how make us better. The pride in thinking we deserve it even if isn't good for us. Which in turn, keeps God from making us even better? It can become a replacement for God.

Pride; the attitude and things we hold onto to make ourselves bigger than God. If we have them we don't need God as much.

Truth is; those things can cause us pain even as we hold on to them. Replacing God with pain is just ridiculous. So why do I do it? Still not sure, but lets all pray for help on this one.

Day 50

Matthew 10:40 & 41 – Be Real

Verse 40 makes me think of how we are to be Jesus to the world. If we act like him, the world will see him. Down side; if we claim to be him and act like idiots, their perception of Jesus may only be given from us. In turn, they will get a bad view of Jesus. When you claim to be a Christian, it comes with great responsibility. I get tired of being good from time to time. I want to scream and yell and tell people what I really think of them. Well, sometimes I do yell a little.

This isn't the point I was thinking about the first read through. As we share Jesus in the best way we can. We shouldn't worry about being good enough. If we are genuine and don't try to be churchy, we will do just fine. Telling them what God has done for you is easy. Don't try to explain the entire Bible. Love them first, tell them what has happened to you personally, them tell them about Jesus. Being genuine is the key. Do it all in Love.

Don't force it. Move forward as you feel lead. Do not move forward out of guilt.

When we share the love, it will not always be received well. If you aren't being rejected, you may not be sharing enough. When we are stepping out we are going to make mistakes and not say the right thing. Even if we say everything right it still might not turn out the way you wish it would. The thing I want you to remember is they are not rejecting you. They are rejecting the Lord. It is still going to hurt, and still make you feel rotten. But I don't want you to live under condemnation. It's going to happen. Remember Jesus was perfect and told thousands about God and showed them perfect Love. Some of them still killed him. Rejection is going to happen; it will usually not be your fault.

Just be real. Be yourself. Don't imitate. Just Love.

Day 51

Matthew 11:4 & 5 – He Will Show You

What I find interesting about this is this. John had baptized Jesus and saw the Lord come down as a dove. He heard the voice of God say that he was his son. He himself declared Jesus the messiah, and here he has sent his followers to find out for sure. The great John the Baptist, had doubt. He knew, but wanted to double check just in case. He's not the first great one to do this. In either case they were not punished, but God gave them the second or third sign and an answer. Look at Gideon; it took three signs from God, before he ended up winning a war with a handful of men. His strategy was, he let God do all the work.

Lesson; if we have times of doubt, ask for help. Ask for Jesus to show himself. The Holy Spirit will show you.

Side note: John didn't have the Holy Spirit. This was before the day of Pentecost. He had faith, but he didn't have the Holy Spirit to speak to him directly when he prayed. We do. We have the Holy Spirit, who will speak to our hearts and show us the truth. We still may doubt. But thank God he forgives our disbelief, and gives us new reasons to believe. For John, he got to hear the stories first hand, of healings, love for the poor, and more.

For us we have the Bible to read and double check our feelings with the truth of God's word. We also have prayer and meditation where we listen. The Holy Spirit can speak to our hearts and encourage us to faith.

Day 52

Matthew 11:6 – Turn to Jesus

6 And tell him, 'God blesses those who do not turn away because of me.'"

Verse 6 is a unique way of saying, Jesus has come to point the way to God. If you accept his message you will be blessed. Jesus did not come to replace God, but to direct us to him. Even today many turn away from God and use Jesus as an excuse. Some claim he is only human, but a really good man. They never believe in him as the savior. Others deny his forgiving power and don't repent. They rely on their own ability to follow rules, rather than Jesus.

A relationship with Jesus brings us closer to God.

You will be blessed when you don't turn away from Jesus, but go to him.

Enough said.

Day 53

Matthew 11:17-19 – Honor the Law

Jesus is pointing out another danger of the law. Remember first, he is the fulfillment of the law, it is his blood that was shed for our sins. There is a penalty for sin. Do not miss this.

But we wrongfully use the law and tradition to gain power over others. In this case they were using the law to try to stop men of God. They twisted the law to fit their needs. The law is perfect and is for God's purpose. It is not for our purpose. There is danger if we use it for our own benefit.

Here they were saying John the Baptist was not of God, because he did not fit into what they thought he should be. Now Jesus isn't either, so there is no way he could be from God.

Closing off your heart because the person isn't what you expect, will cause you to miss a blessing. Using the law to hold someone else down and to tell others not to listen to them, you are danger of a sin that will separate you from God.

When we use the law for our own purpose, we are trying to be God. This is the original sin, which leads to death. We can however repent. If we get too deep into this deception, the chances of repentance grow less. Not impossible, but less likely.

Are you using your own feelings as gospel? Are you judging others with rules that you yourself haven't mastered. Or maybe judging people with personal standards, that can't be supported by the Bible?

If we are judging others, then we are not honoring the perfect law of God. This does not mean we take everything that comes our way. But we must be careful not to judge on our own standards.

Day 54

Matthew 11:23&24 – Repent or be Doomed

23 "And you people of Capernaum, will you be honored in heaven? No, you will go down to the place of the dead. For if the miracles I did for you had been done in wicked Sodom, it would still be here today.
24 I tell you, even Sodom will be better off on judgment day than you." NLT

Jesus is making a point. He is telling the people who have begged for a sign, "Here's your sign."
"I gave you signs and miracles, yet you still do not believe."

The danger here is in comparing ourselves with others. If we think we are doing better than others and therefore we are OK, we are in big trouble. Here the people of Capernaum were complacent with there religious position and viewed themselves as better than Romans, Samaritans, and the rest of the world. They were able to claim the promise of Israel. They were the chosen people after all. Jesus is taking that false security away. If they do not except Jesus, then the doom is coming. If they do not repent, eternity will be bad, really bad.

If we avoid Repentance and claim anything else as sufficient, we are living a lie, and are doomed, as well.

This was the true point. They didn't want to repent. They only wanted the blessing.

Sorry, it doesn't work that way.

Repent, Believe, and then Be Blessed.

Day 55

Matthew 11:25 & 26 – Begins with Humility

25 "At that time Jesus prayed this prayer: "O Father, Lord of heaven and earth, thank you for hiding these things from those who think themselves wise and clever, and for revealing them to the childlike.
26 Yes, Father, it pleased you to do it this way!" NLT

This is not meant to be a dig at you people that are smarter than I am.

It isn't about intellect.

It **is** about those who think they are smarter than God.
God hid the truth from those whose egos were so big they didn't need God. His message was for the humble. The truth is; it still is. Our whole salvation starts with humility. Without humility there is no salvation.

How is this?

Easy, Salvation cannot happen without repentance. No one will repent until they realize they actually need help. Pride keeps them from asking for help. SO it all starts with humility.

It's ok to be a failure and sinner, as long as we are humble enough to admit our failures and repent.

If you are humble and know you need help, then the word of the Lord is just for you.

People with egos have a hard time in church and understanding what the Lord is doing. They often, if not always, miss the very work of the Lord right around them.

Day 56

Matthew 11:29 – Jesus' yoke starts with the Word

29 "Take my yoke upon you. Let me teach you, because I am humble and gentle at heart, and you will find rest for your souls. 30 For my yoke is easy to bear, and the burden I give you is light." NLT

There is another truth here; it is that following Jesus is the easiest way to go through life. The ups and downs are still there, but having the Holy Spirit to help you through. He has even helped me avoid more downs than I deserve. It doesn't always keep me from being grumpy, but I bounce back quick. Some of my co-workers may argue the quick part.

Yet we find ourselves afraid to follow him. How can we be so scared to do the very thing that is best for us? Instead we listen to the lies that come into our heart. We don't build our faith.

Building our faith is the only defense to unbelief. Faith is the opposite of worry and fear. So if we are afraid of following Jesus, we need to build our Faith.

Faith is built on the Word of God. This is the only thing that builds it. It's not singing, listening to Christian music, it is by reading the Word. Take time to have your own personal study of the word. This book can be an aid, but remember it is to be used with the Bible open and reading even more than I point out. This is why I don't always have the scripture at the top of the page. Take what I have here each day and look for cross-references where what I am saying is found somewhere else. Don't just take my word for it. Finding more scripture verses that support what I say will encourage you even more.

Taking on his yoke starts with the Word.

Day 57

Matthew 12:7 & 8 – Mercy Over Task

There was a long list of things to do from the Old Testament that we can do to please God.

Things like; Keeping the Sabbath, Burning Sacrifices, and many more. These are things that we can do, and for the most part they are not that hard. Doing nothing on Saturday is just that doing nothing. I love doing that. The law is a list of things that we can accomplish on or own. With a little will power, we can do it just fine.

However to please God is all about attitude.

Bad attitude means all the work is worthless.

Part of this attitude is our attitude towards others.

Jesus mentions Micah 6:6 *"I want you to show love, not offer sacrifices. I want you to know me more than I want burnt offerings." NLT*

Jesus is telling us that Mercy is way more important than any task. More important than the work we do.

Mercy over Tasks

Loving others, **Forgiving** others, being **Kind** to others, and being **Gentle** to others.

Jesus goes on to tell in verse 8 that he can use the rules in any way he needs to, to show mercy.

The RULES were never meant to over shadow LOVE.

LOVE over RULES.   RULE with LOVE.

Day 58

Matthew 12:13 – No Step by Step

Verse 13 is Jesus healing of a man with a crippled hand. Jesus looks at the man and says, "Hold out your hand." NLT

This is no surprise to any of us. He is capable of healing and healed almost everyone he came in contact with.

My thought for the day is that he healed a lot of people, but he didn't do it the same way twice. At least not that is recorded. He healed so many times that wasn't written down, I think most of the time it was a simple word or touch from Jesus' hand.

What I see is a pattern set up for us to live by, a step by step on proper use of Faith. If we follow these steps, our every prayer will be answered.

First you need faith.
Next you go to Jesus.
Then.....

You may need to jump in a pool, pick up a mat, go to a priest, stand up, or what ever Jesus instructs us to do.

Step 3 is **Listen** to the Holy Spirit on what we need to do.

See step three is different in every situation. It changes with the person, the time, the need.

There is no ritual, or step by step method to get what you want.

This is a sure thing, Jesus wants to help you. He is there for you. The way he helps you will be a surprise.

Faith, Jesus, Listen, Do.

Day 59

Matthew 12:30 – Give or Against

30 "Anyone who isn't with me opposes me, and anyone who isn't working with me is actually working against me." NLT

Verse 30 tells us not only do we need to be on Jesus' side, but also not against him. So to say church is good for someone else, but not for me, is the same as being against God. Even if you never say that you have a problem with Jesus. Even if you don't think you do. If you do not support him, you are against him.

If we do not Love others as he has asked us to, then we are against him.

If we do not give our Tithe (10% of our income) to the local church, we are actually against him.

HOW?

1. God gives a vision to the pastor and the elders for that church. This is a special way that the church will reach out to the community and the lost. (If your church is not, pray about finding one that does. But follow the leading of the Spirit on the church you should be in.)
If you are in a church with a biblical vision, the vision needs money to do what it is to do. This is not a bad thing. God will provide the funds.

2. The funds will mostly come from the members, as it should. If you or I do not give to the church, we are not helping.

3. By not giving we not only don't help, but say indirectly that we do not believe in the vision and mission of the church.

4. The Vision is from God, so if we don't believe in the vision, we are then against his vision.

As I came home from church I was praying that the Lord would give a verse about tithe. Without hunting it down, there it was, the next verse in our series. It was God's appointed time for this message.

If we do not Tithe, we are showing that we do not support or care about the work that God has for the local church. We can say we do but the proof is in the pudding.

I have been guilty as of late (recently I didn't) of not giving my full tithe. I caught up tonight. I had to apologize to the church for my unbelief. I was holding on because of fear of not having enough. Jesus is enough. I have seen him provide over and over again. But even I have to over come fear and give anyway. Jesus' return is amazing. Do not fear the giving. Embrace it and see how God will honor it and bless you in return in ways you could never expect or imagine.

Tithing can be found in: Malachi 3:10, 2 chronicles 31:6, Gen 28:22, Hebrews 7:5

Luke 11:42, is not an excuse to not tithe.

Parted Waters

I'm gonna praise you for the parted waters,
    You got me to the other side.
I'm gonna shout for the parted waters,
    I'm dancing here safe and dry.

The Jordan River and the big Red Sea.
You split them open in a time of need.
One gave freedom, and one gave land,
Both met a promise, both by your hand.
Today's the same, you still hold the waves.
Parting the troubles blocking our way.

I'm gonna praise you for the parted waters,
    And the testimony that you give.
I'm gonna shout for the parted waters,
    In your victory is where I live.

Day 60

Matthew 12:31 – Unforgiveable Sin

Verse 31 tells us to not worry about the past even if we did something against Jesus. He will forgive if we repent, just as he forgave those who killed him. He said just before he died, "Forgive them for they know not what they do." The good thing is he forgives us even when we know what we are doing.

Jesus doesn't hold anything we do before we get to know him against us. We don't get to know him until the Holy Spirit draws us to him. It is the Holy Spirit that shows us our need for forgiveness. It is the Holy Spirit that brings us to Jesus. It is still our responsibility to do the asking. It is still us that must humble ourselves to the point of asking for forgiveness. SO, there is nothing he won't forgive. Almost. Blasphemy or speaking against the Holy Spirit is not forgivable.

What?

To understand we need to look back at the role of the Holy Spirit. He tells us that we need Jesus. If we reply with a no, we deny the truth he is telling us. This is like telling him he's a liar. If we deny what the Spirit is telling us in our hearts, we are denying our need for Jesus. If we do not humble ourselves and admit we need repentance, we do not get forgiveness. Without repentance and Jesus there is no gift of eternal life with God. This means no heaven.

Therefore the sin that is not forgivable is the sin of pride, and not humbling ourselves as the Holy Spirit is prompting us to.

Jesus doesn't hold our sins against him against us, but it doesn't take away the fact we need him and his forgiveness, through his Blood.

Forgiveness only comes after we ask for it.

Day 61

Matthew 12:33 – Good Fruit

Verse 33 talks about the good fruit of a Christian. I think my fruit is almost good with just a few bruises.

I'm not sure if I could give an accurate account for my fruit. I have always been one, to criticize myself more than others do. I feel my good fruit is rare. I could easily tell you every wrong word, every sneer, every bad thing I said, and much, much more.

As we walk with the Lord, it is important to read his Word regularly, to better our fruit. We have fruit, some good and some bad. As we read his word and apply it to our own life, we start to replace our bad fruit with good fruit. Others will begin to see the better fruit. I hope you will see it to. I myself, don't always. When I think I have a good piece of fruit, I tell others about it and that puts a bruise on it. But if you cut it into pieces, there is still some that is good.

We should all strive to have good fruit, and we can only have good fruit with Jesus' help, and by the guidance of the Holy Spirit. Don't let yourself get bogged down by self examination. Just live for God and move forward. While I think about it, I don't let it slow down my ministry. I could let my guilt keep me from writing this devotional. From what I have heard, this would not be a good thing.

Good fruit is Love, Patience, Kindness, and Gentleness. I am really good at all of these a couple times a week, now if I could just do it more often. It will get better, if I keep getting closer to God.

Day 62

Matthew 12:37 – Watch Your Tongue

37 "The words you say will either acquit you or condemn you."
NLT

Are we careful about what we say? Do we say things with little care of how they will effect the other person? Do we use our words to hurt someone else?

There are times we say things that hurt, without actually meaning to hurt them. There are times we do it on purpose. There are times we just don't think.

Jesus tells us to use our words for Good. Good meaning to use them to help and lift up people. If we say things without thinking, it is carelessness, which isn't much better than the deliberate attack.

I wish I could say I never say anything without thinking. This would be a lie. If people knew what I do filter, they would see how much a do restrain myself. But I still have a long way to go.

The truth is, when I say something mean or hurtful, unfortunately I do mean it. This doesn't mean I don't feel bad. I usually regret it quickly. I would say that it usually follows by myself being hurt.

Getting even with words or actions still causes pain. The world is filled with Pain. We need to do whatever we can to stop or temper the pain. Even for those who don't deserve it. I measure my walk with the Lord, by showing love with those who don't deserve it. This means showing mercy. Our own salvation is because of Mercy. Without mercy, we are all doomed.

Lord, help me today watch my tongue and say gentle and kind words.

Day 63

Matthew 12:48-50 – Don't Limit God

48 "Jesus asked, "Who is my mother? Who are my brothers?" 49Then he pointed to his disciples and said, "Look, these are my mother and brothers. 50Anyone who does the will of my Father in heaven is my brother and sister and mother!" NLT

Here Jesus is stopping something that still goes on today. Denying others claims against him.

Jesus died for everyone. Good, Bad, Black, White, Young, Old, etc.

Here they are trying to confine Jesus and his calling by linking him to one family. "He's just a man from Nazareth, and here is his earthly family." Same as saying, "He's just a man." But he is so much more. Today he can't be claimed by one race, or another. Pictures of Jesus as a white man are just one example. Jesus doesn't belong to any one person or group. He is not ownable. He is the creator. We are his. Now there is nothing wrong with saying, "My Jesus", as long as we don't claim him to limit him or his power.

He gave us instructions not to make carvings or pictures of him. No one knows what he looked like. Not important. He is not confined to a body. He is the Savior and God.

The most popular way to claim Jesus is through denominations.

Jesus wasn't Catholic. He isn't Baptist; He's not even Assembly of God. He is more than a denomination can explain, or define.

Don't limit God. Reach out to him, and he will touch you. He is everything you need. Limit him; you limit his ability to help you. Be open to ALL Jesus and the Holy Spirit has for you.

Day 64

Matthew 13:3 & 4 – Hard Hearts

3 "Listen! A farmer went out to plant some seeds. 4 As he scattered them across his field, some seeds fell on a footpath, and the birds came and ate them." NLT

Many have hearts that are hardened. The word of God comes to them and it never takes root. The word is taken away and replaced with lies.

This is sad but true.

We are to be the farmer. Not just throwing the seed on fertile soil, but to all the ground. We do need to spread it mostly on the soil that is ready and will use it. But we are not the ones to judge who should hear it. So we need to tell everyone about Jesus. Let the word be spread. Let the Holy Spirit do as he sees fit. Let the people hear it and decide for themselves to follow Jesus or not.

Only God knows who is ready. SO we need to spread the word. Let it fly. Then let God deal with the hearts it lands on.

The Birds may come and take it away, but we will be honored and blessed for the effort.

Day 65

Matthew 13:8 & 9 – Fertile Soil

As you read these words of the Lord, you have a choice. You can read them for understanding. The Holy Spirit will bring to light the understanding you need, in how it applies to you. I share what the verses mean to me. I share what the Spirit has reveled to me.

Remember this. My words are not as important as the words in the Bible. It is important to read the Word of God for yourself and listen to the Holy Spirit.

When we read the Word, we need to look at it, listen in our heart for the Holy Spirit.

I took a long time off, until I started to write the devotional, but I used to write my thoughts and what I learned from each verse. It was a way to visualize what was going on in my heart.

Sometimes I would just write a few words on the side edges of my bible. Other times, I would write it in a note book. Either way, think about what the words mean and what he was trying to say to us.

Being fertile is not just the listening, the rocky ground did that. But it is staying in the word. If we stay in the word, the word of God will take root and grow into a life style of living for the Lord.

See, it all starts with the Word of God, which is the Bible.
Read it.
Listen
Stay in it.

The Holy Spirit will bring the understanding.

Day 66

Matthew 13:12 – Listen with Faith

Jesus used Parables so normal everyday people could understand the Kingdom of God. The religious leaders, much like today, made it hard. The harder they made it to understand, the better for them. They wanted to make sure the people looked to them for understanding instead of looking to God. They often used big words and talked over their heads. The pretense was that the people needed them to understand God's will, and any chance to get to heaven.

Jesus actually talks very plainly. He spoke so plainly that the religious leaders didn't understand. Not because they weren't able to, but because they don't really listen. Maybe they mumble under their breath, "that ridiculous" or "that's not possible".

What do we think or hear others say about God today?

God doesn't care. God doesn't listen? That's impossible. That doesn't happen any more. If this is what you hear, don't listen. These are lies.

It is hard to believe but thousands of people go to church every week, without really listening to what was being said. They hear the words, but they hear them without FAITH.

Without faith, the words have no bite. They have no meaning. They are simply nice words that don't apply to them.

Without Faith the words have no power.

Day 67

Matthew 13:24 – Watch out for Lies

I am going to stick with just the first three verses of the parable of the farmer. As in many of the parables, they are simple yet complex. They can have several meanings baked into one. That is why I encourage you **not** to skip over parables you think you've read so many times they are no longer relevant. The truth is that the Holy Spirit can bring new life to any verse. He can bring to light a truth about God, at the perfect time, when you really need it.

Verse 24 thru 26 starts the parable with the planting of good seed. This seed represents God's word again. As we share it and tell it, we need to realize the enemy (Devil) will sneak in and plant lies. The devil's only offense is lying about the truth. He has no truth in him. God is the only truth and God is no longer with the devil.

Let there be no doubt about it. The lies will follow. We need to continue to share the Word. It is more powerful by far. We also need to encourage others to read the Word daily.

We know the only weapon the Devil has and we know our best and only defense; The WORD (Truth).

The WORD is a two edged sword. It cuts through any lie, even our own. Hebrews 4:12

In this context, it is a two edged weed whacker.

Day 68

Matthew 13:31 – Faith can Grow

31 "Here is another illustration Jesus used: "The Kingdom of Heaven is like a mustard seed planted in a field. 32 It is the smallest of all seeds, but it becomes the largest of garden plants; it grows into a tree, and birds come and make nests in its branches." NLT

Verse 31 brings us to the parable of the mustard seed. This is a popular verse and has a lot of truth to it. More often than not, it is a verse that is loved, but not always believed. I mean what can the Faith of a Mustard Seed do? Truth is it can do a lot.

Remember it is the Holy Spirit that is doing the hard part. All we have to do is pray and believe. Believing is kind of hard, at times, like when you walk out of the church and get in your car.

We are here again at the word Faith. As I have said before, Faith is obtained through the Bible. Read it and the Mustard seed will begin to grow. This growth is the growth of faith. As you pray and see God do his thing, you will have more faith to believe in bigger things. This continues to grow just as the tree from a simple seed. The growth is not just in Faith, but it is growth in miracles. Signs of God's grace and power follow our faith. The more faith we have and show, the bigger God's work in our lives. Tonight I prayed with someone that was healed. I saw for the first time, a physical miracle happen while I prayed. While I was following the Spirit's direction, my friend Alfonzo was there in agreement. Working together to encourage each other's faith.

As God becomes more evident in our lives, people will be drawn to the Love of Jesus, just as the birds nest in the mustard tree.

Don't be afraid to grow. Embrace it and read the word, build your faith, and watch what God **CAN** do, through you.

Day 69

Matthew 13:33 – Little Bit of Heaven

33 "The Kingdom of Heaven is like the yeast a woman used in making bread. Even though she put only a little yeast in three measures of flour, it permeated every part of the dough." NLT

Yeast.

Yeast is a small fungi used to make bread rise. It is small and only takes a pinch to effect the whole dough. When the dough is kneaded, it doesn't have to be worked hard to make sure the yeast is in every part. It just seems to work its way through on its own.

So the Kingdom of Heaven is like that?

I am not sure what Jesus meant. What I was reminded of tonight is the touch of the Holy Spirit. We don't have a touch everyday. We don't have a touch or miracle every week. I know that the Spirit is close to me every minute of every day, but the truth is we can't always see or feel it. Today we visited a church and the pastor talked about Mary. She pointed out that even she didn't talk to God every day. She had to be reminded, because after Jesus was born and the shepherds and wise men were gone, Jesus was just a baby. Then she had more babies. Life gets busy. Nothing is said again until Jesus is twelve. He's not lost. He's with his true father. Again she takes the experience and hides it in her heart.

For us it may seem like years since our last experience. But that one or two encounters with God changes our lives forever. This change stays with us for the rest of our lives. These few miraculous encounters are small in comparison, to the number of hours in our lives. It is just like the yeast filling the whole loaf of bread, Jesus fills our whole life with his mercy and love.

These encounters are little bits of Heaven.

I can't wait until we are in his presence all the time.

Day 70

Matthew 13:47-51 – Don't Fear the Net

47 "Again, the Kingdom of Heaven is like a fishing net that was thrown into the water and caught fish of every kind.
48 When the net was full, they dragged it up onto the shore, sat down, and sorted the good fish into crates, but threw the bad ones away.
49 That is the way it will be at the end of the world. The angels will come and separate the wicked people from the righteous,
50 throwing the wicked into the fiery furnace, where there will be weeping and gnashing of teeth. 51 Do you understand all these things?" NLT

Verse 47 tells us about the Net of Judgment. This is the end of our days when the Lord brings us before himself. But not all will be allowed to enter heaven.

There is only one way to heaven at that is through Jesus. Humbling ourselves and repenting of our sin is the only way we can have our sins removed. Without this removal, we are considered wicked. We will be thrown away as a bad fish. We are found to be wicked, if and only if, we refuse to repent. Heaven is possible to anyone who believes and repents.

We have no need to fear the day of the net, if we have repented and have put our trust in Jesus and his blood.

We need **NOT** fear it, but we do need to understand Hell is a real situation.

The Good New is we can go to Heaven. Don't go there alone.

Day 71

Matthew 13:55-58 – Rejected

I am going to start the Christmas Season with a reminder. Jesus was rejected even before the Cross. In fact he was rejected over and over again. He was even rejected by the very ones he helped and people that saw Jesus heal others.

Here he is being rejected by those who watched him grow up. Since Jesus was perfect, I find it hard to believe they didn't think he was special. Jealousy was probably very high. How could any kid measure up to Jesus? This had to make several parents a little jealous. Okay, a lot jealous.

Today Jesus is rejected by many. Now more than ever people avoid saying Christmas.

The chosen People of Israel still do not accept Jesus, yet are looking forward to his return. (They think for the first time)

He has been rejected, and even though he knew the rejection was coming, Jesus still came. He came to the cross. He came to a broken earth. He set aside all he knew about our failures and our Sin and he came anyway. He came into a cold world, both in temperature and in heart.

So I start this Holiday Christmas season, with a heavy heart for those who do not know Jesus as I do. I have a heavy heart for these who are hurting and still reject the one who can heal their hurts. They reject the one who can change their lives forever. And I mean forever.

Day 72

Matthew 14:16 – Stress

Jesus has just preached for hours to a crowd of 5000 men, so that would be 10,000 plus for all the people. Even after hours of teaching the people weren't watching their watches or sneaking out the back to get a good seat at the local eatery. Jesus takes a break and the Disciples are faced with a problem. They are afraid they will be stuck with feeding them, even though Jesus is clearly in charge.

Ever find yourself in this position?

For example; someone has just been assigned a task at work and you just know you will be stuck doing the hard part of it, or stuck with the clean up. Maybe some one at church starts pushing for a new system or organization of a ministry. You just know that you will be the one hit with the new responsibility, when you clearly don't have time to mess with it. Sometimes we're right and sometimes we are not. Either way we are quick to worry about what might happen. When has stress ever helped any situation? Fact is; stress never actually helps, it only makes it worse. While stress may not affect the out come directly, it can affect the way we feel and respond to the situation.

Isn't this what shows our character? Isn't this what shows we are different in Christ? Not the ability to avoid situations, but how we handle them. I know this to be true, because I am horrible at not getting stressed. There are some situations I am amazing at, like being surrounded by 40 little kids and keeping them in line and not losing my mind. I am not so cool at work, dealing with adults that act like little kids and the constant need to babysit them. This is when I get stressed out.

Look at what Jesus says to them, "It isn't necessary..." See, it isn't necessary to get worked up and send everyone home in a panic. If they did this, they would be undoing everything Jesus had done.

Matthew – Jesus Speaks

Isn't it just like Jesus to look at us and say, "just do it." Don't look at all the parts of the situation that can't happen or won't work. Just move forward with what you have and not worry about what you don't. Once we step out in faith God can make the miraculous happen. But we first must step forward.

Stress – Get over it.

Day 73

The Way God Sees Us

As I pulled into our churches parking lot, I saw two Master Commission students in their second year. I watched them walking and I knew their names. I knew what an awesome blessing they were to me and the church last year. I remembered something about their testimony that they shared at their graduation from year one back in May. I was trying to remember what it was, they were delivered from. I remember that the testimonies were surprising, and very incredible. Until then I though they were two girls that grew up in church and never did anything wrong. I had only seen them as polite nice girls that served God with all their heart. So as I watched them before I got a clear picture of their testimony, I gave up trying.

It was God who told me to stop trying. "Why do you need to know?" I heard him say to my heart. I didn't. When I look at these two beautiful women of God, I still see polite nice girls that serve God with all their hearts. As I thought about it, I realize that this is how God sees us.

He knows what we have done. He was there when we did it. But when we repent and confess our sins, God forgets. He forgets on purpose. He chooses not to remember. Now all he sees is men and women of God who serve him and love him.

We shouldn't see ourselves any different. Repent and forget what we used to do. We have to choose to forget. Every time you think about it. Stop! Thank God for the forgiveness. You don't have to ask him to forgive you again. He already did. So just thank him and get your mind on the goodness of God. Put on some music, read the bible, or what ever it takes to get in a positive frame of mind.

God sees you as a FORGIVEN, PERSON OF GOD, FAMILY, and CLEAN.

Day 74

Matthew 14:18 – Little or a lot

Bring them here, is Jesus' reply to the disciples saying they didn't have enough. I can see if this was me, I would have taken the 2 fish and 5 loaves of bread to Jesus only to make my point that there was nothing they had to offer. Isn't it funny how that is? It seems like one or two is much better than zero to prove a point. "Look here it is. What can you possibly do with it? Give it to the first 2 people and then make everyone else mad and cause a riot?" If we sat and thought about it, we could come up with a lot more excuses, or a list of bad things that will happen for even trying. I'll spare us of this negative exercise.

God can make things out of nothing. He is really good at it. But I think what God loves best, is to take a little and do amazing things with it. Look at me, I am little, but he has done some really cool things through me. It's always in a way that I can't take credit for it. That's his little joke on me. But it is still awesome to be used, or be apart of a miracle.

So if you want to be part of a miracle this week or even today, give God your little and watch him work. What is your little?

MONEY – to ministry or your local church,
TIME – Friends, neighbor, elderly on your block, church, ministry, or mentoring.
HOME – Host a bible study, dinner party, invite someone new to the church or neighborhood.
TALENT – Don't worry if you think others are better. Give the talent you enjoy to God. Paint a wall for the nursery, join the choir, write letters to the people who have been out. Write letters to a soldier over seas. Bake cookies for people in the hospital or in the waiting room of the ICU unit, whether you know them or not. Take some food to the Fire Department.

What are you good at? DO IT.

Day 75

Matthew 14:27 – Take Courage

Verse 27 is Jesus' first words to his disciples as he approached the boat. He is of course walking on the water. At this point some of them were calling him a ghost. Peter has not yet jumped into or onto the water. Something to remember about the disciples, they were not all sailors. While some were fishermen like Peter and John, most were not. So when the seas were not calm, neither were they. Even before they saw Jesus coming to them on the water in the midst of the storm, they were scared. Seeing a person floating on top of the water just added to that fear.

Jesus did as he usually did, kept it simple. "Don't be afraid."

It is the second half of his proclamation that stuck to me tonight. No matter where we are. No matter what we face. No matter how much pain we are in. No matter how far past hope we think we have gotten. We can and must hold on to these 5 words. These 5 words can get us through anything. These 5 words can give us the faith to stay when everything else is telling us to run and hide.

"Take Courage, I am Here!"

This is as true today as it was that day so many years ago. The Holy Spirit, our ultimate comforter, is right here and right where you are. So Today;

TAKE COURAGE. HE IS HERE!

We have no reason to fear. Jesus and his Spirit are here and will always be here. Call to him, just as Peter did. Take courage. At work, He is there. At the family get together, He is there. At home, He is there. At the Bank He is there. Even at church, he is there. No matter where you are or what you face, HE is there.

Take Courage!

Day 76

Matthew 14:29 – Jump In

29 "Yes, come," Jesus said. NLT

We can often leave the focus on Peter sinking, and there is good example of how we should keep our eyes on God, but that's not what's standing out to me.

Peter is blown away by the fact Jesus is walking on the water. Like so many of the kids I teach.

"MY TURN! MY TURN!"

Or like me and my friends,
"That was so COOL! Can I try? Come on man let me do it."

Peter wanted to get out there and do something not only cool, but that also defies Physics. It was impossible, but as the scripture says "All things are possible..." but how many of us actually believe that enough to jump out of the boat?

Jumping at the right time and walking with wisdom is a balance that can only come through study of his Word, Prayer, and listening to the Leading of the Holy Spirit. I say this because I don't want anyone going out and jumping off a building to see if they can fly.

What Peter did right is:
    He desired to be like Jesus. = Dream (Hope)
    He asked God if he could. = Prayer
    He Jumped to it. = Faith in Action.
    Sank = Messed up
    Called on Jesus = Repent
    Pulled to safety = Forgiven.

Prayer is not just a one time thing. We need to pray and ask God for help all the time and every time we slip and sink. Our journey doesn't stop with the first victory, and our life will not be complete with only one victory. There will be times in ALL of our lives that we will mess up and sink. We **can** repent and get pulled back to safety, to continue our journey. As we know from Peter's life was just one of many miracles and moments he would be part of.

So for us, we too can do amazing things through Christ.

What's your dream for your life? Pray for help, guidance, and permission. When you here Jesus say "YES, COME." don't wait, jump into the sea and start walking. Remember to keep your eyes on Jesus and don't be scared. The wind and waves are still going to be there, but they can't take you down if you keep on walking.

When Jesus says, Come, there is no failure in him.

Day 77

Matthew 14:31 – Don't Doubt

It is a mystery to me what would be worse, sinking and failing in front of all my friends, or the fear of dying while getting all wet. Then there is that small part of having to face the one you wanted to impress so badly, and not be seen as a failure.

If it was me, the cold water, the fear, the cry out for help, and the dripping wet clothes, would be enough for me to know I had messed up. The last thing I would need is for Jesus to point it out. In a way I can see this as cruel punishment, but Jesus is right. There was no real reason to worry. Peter got in the boat, and was humbled.

Do you know anyone that would have started with the excuses?

"Did you see that gust of wind? It knocked me right off my feet. I wouldn't have fallen if it wasn't for that wind. It was at least hurricane category 2 winds. I'll do it again right now. I didn't see you out there. Man, I was about to drowned what would you have done?"

Excuses are good for making us feel better, for about 3 to 4 seconds. But when we are facing Jesus face to face, and he asks "Why did you doubt?" what will we say? Truth is there are no excuses. He not only knows the whole story, but he knows the motive. He knows exactly why we failed.

The only thing we can do is be humble, and tell him we are sorry.

Why did we doubt? We do it all the time. Jesus always wants what is best for us. We have nothing to worry about, even when the wind is blowing like a hurricane.

If you start to sink, call to Jesus and he will pull you back up.

Day 78

Matthew 15:3-6 – Serving God or Serving Self

Verse 3 starts a lecture to the religious leaders, who have used religion to get what they want. They continually used the name of God for self gain. The example given is neglecting the family or parents, for what was claimed to be for a vow. Making a promise to God that would hurt your family is not in the will of God. Using the name of the Lord for self preservation or to gain wealth or power is even worse than that.

As we work in the church and in our ministries, we must continue everyday to lift up God. God has to be the center and the focus of every move we make. The minute we take our ministry down a path of pride and power, we start a journey that will hurt people. More people in fact than we ever thought possible to help. These types of hurts will not be easily healed. So even if we started in the ministry to help people, our ministry can turn into a hurting force.

I am reminding each of us, how easily we can go from serving God to serving ourselves, and the hurt that can follow. Decisions we make must line up with God's word. So it is important to READ the word, so we'll know if we are following it. Pray for wisdom, and pray for his will.

God's will is so much more important than our own agenda. After all it's part of the Lord's Prayer which is important. It is also in the Bible not just a Catholic tradition. It is something we should all be following. Our agenda must be God's agenda. His agenda may be challenging at times, but it is always for our good and the Church body's good. What is good for us alone is not good for the body and can hurt it. Hurting the body hurts us.

I love God and his guidance.

Day 79

Matthew 15:7 – Selfish Hypocrites

The point of this lesson is simple. Jesus knows our motives. He takes our motives very seriously, and so should we.

Right after God and our Spouse comes the Church Body. Our lives should be lived to lift up God and be edifying to the Church Body. Selfishness keeps that from happening. Selfishness over titles, space, friendships, or attention, can lead to stress, anger, and bitterness. None of these feelings are healthy for your ministry or the Church Body.

I'm not so much pointing out the slips we have from time to time. Those are easily repented of and go as fast as they come. But I am pointing out the Bitterness and Un-forgiveness that have been dragged around for years. The hindrances that keep the Love of Jesus from flowing and the Bitterness is rooted in selfishness. Bitter over a situation that didn't go the way we thought it should have gone. Or even gone the way we felt we deserved it to go. When our conversations with others are filled with statements on what we deserved or how we've been done wrong, is unhealthy selfishness.

God has things in place that will happen for a better outcome than we can see. If we pull out early and get bitter of the process, we miss out. Our beef is not with the person we are blaming. It is with God. God's control is perfect. He does not allow others to affect our lives, jobs, or family, for no reason. He means for ALL things to work out for the GOOD of those who love him. If we stop believing this and get bitter, we become Hypocrites, and our ministry suffers and we stop working for the Lord with our whole heart. Our worship becomes empty. This leads to turning our back on Jesus totally, if forgiveness is not asked for and accepted.

There is redemption. We must first start with HUMILITY and REPENTANCE. After that let the healing begin.

Day 80

Matthew 15:10 – Words Can Hurt

Sticks and stones may break my bones but words will never hurt me.

We all were taught this as a child. As a parent we wish that it was true, which we know the words have no truth behind them. We wish they wouldn't hurt, but the reality is not much hurts more than words. Broken bones heal a lot faster.

Words can break a heart, cause stress, confuse a mind, and scar ones feelings.

Here Jesus was pointing out that the religious people were very concerned about what they and others ate, but gave little regard to what they said. Jesus is making it very clear that our words are very important. I have had on many occasions the privilege of saying the right thing at the right time. This has only happened when I was guided by the Holy Spirit. In these times healing and encouragement takes place. When I tell people what I think without praying about it first, I usually causes harm.

Walking in the Spirit is important when it comes to not sticking our foot in our mouth. When we do say harmful things a simple sorry does not always make it go away.

It takes more than words to gain respect, it takes action. It takes action and words to begin the healing process. But it only takes a few words to undo all the good, and lose respect. It's not a fair situation, but a true one. So we must be careful.

Prayer and reading God's word daily helps. Asking God for wisdom in the words we use is a great way to start each day. Taking deep breaths before speaking and thinking before speaking, helps prevent harm as well.

Let's agree to be less harmful today.

Day 81

Matthew 15:13 – Dreams

Jesus' reply to the disciples was a warning of the Pharisees being upset. I will let you read that part for yourself. What struck me right away was the plant being uprooted if it is not planted by God. A Vision that are not built on God's word is planted by us, therefore it will be uprooted.

Visions are plans we see in our heart or head, that we desire to come true. SO you could call it our dreams. The dreams we have that are rooted in our relationship with Jesus, are the ones that last forever.

The great thing is that the dreams we have as a result of God's Grace and Love are the best. They are the best for us and the best for others. Dreams from our own desires are rooted in our own selfishness. Selfishness closes the dream to others and uses others instead of helping others. These selfish dreams do not find success for long. When they do find success, they do not bring satisfaction. They fill us with a desire for more, more selfish desire and want.

Why are so many filthy rich people so miserable? They have empty dreams that money doesn't fulfill. The more they get the more they need. The more they need, the more stress and misery they have.

Dreams that God has blessed, bring Joy and Satisfaction, not only at completion, but all along the way. Following God in your journey to your dreams brings joy and new mercy every morning.

What's your dream? Does it come from your love for God or does it find root in Selfishness?

Find your dream and then dream it?

Day 82

Matthew 15:24-28 – He Will Give You More

At first it looks like Jesus is trying to deny her the forgiveness she is looking for. How could Jesus do that? Is he discriminating? Is he a racist? Of course not, He himself told the disciples to go and make disciples of ALL men.

We must look at the whole dialog. We must also remember Jesus knows us better than we know ourselves. He is God and knew what she would say to the questions he asked.

The edification of the Church Body is always on his mind. He gives us testimonies and allows us to go through experiences, not only to build our faith, but also to build the faith of those around us. He is going to bless us, and he is going to help us, but he will do it in a way that will get the most 'bang for the buck'. Why do everything in private? When he can help several have a break through with each moment or miracle.

In this case, he could have told the crowd, about faith, but he also loves to use us. Now that Jesus is back in heaven, it's how he works; through us. When you find yourself wondering why God has allowed you to get in a hard situation, have **faith**. Jesus will help you through it if you look to him for help. And when he does, it will be a great day for you in the building of your faith. It will also give you a new and unique testimony that will reach many others.

I am reminded of the parable about sowing seeds. Just like a little seed produces 100's of times more seed, one testimony shared with others, while pointing to and glorying God, will harvest faith like a field of wheat.

Don't hold back. Tell your testimony, and look for the next one. You have another one right around the corner. The more you share, the more Jesus will give you. We must be good stewards as the man with 10 talents. If we prove faithful with the one, he will give us two.

Day 83

Matthew 15:32 – Your Little is Much

34 Jesus asked, "How much bread do you have?" NLT

At this point in the Story, Jesus has just taught for three days and the 4000 men were out of food. The disciples had already forgotten how Jesus feed the 5000 with only a hand full of food. Here they are distressed to find Jesus asking them to help them once again. He was always doing that. I believe this was not the way the disciple wanted to live. What about them? When will they get to eat in peace? When will they get to leave at the end of the service and relax? But I babble on again.

Jesus asks them one simple question, he asks of us today. "How much do you have?"

When we find ourselves in situations we don't think we can get through, or perhaps a new direction the Lord has called us to, he's not asking us to tell him what we can't do. He already knows your weaknesses. In fact, he knows the weaknesses we don't think are weaknesses, and he knows the strengths we have that we would call weak. We may even think it's nothing important. God knows how to use us and our weaknesses. He also is the master at using our strengths in such a way that people are touched in life changing ways.

Here we all stand at a possible new starting point. What do you have? Jesus has a plan for your "little" to use it in a miraculous way. Miracles happen and will happen, through his people that have called on his name. Those who have humbled themselves in repentance and now have a new birth in Jesus. A ministry that maybe ready for a new level or a ministry that is ready to just begin. This year can be a miraculous year, if you hold out your "little" and offer it to Jesus.

You can be a life changer.

Day 84

Matthew 16:2 – Seeing isn't Believing

Here we go, people making demands of God. Of course they didn't believe Jesus was God and didn't think he would be able to do anything. Miracles come from Faith. If there is no faith then there is no miracle. Demanding the miracle first, then I'll believe, is backwards.

As much as I would like to believe the saying, "Seeing is Believing." It is just not true. Ask an Alabama fan if Auburn is number one, and see what they believe. They saw them beat Oregon. You may hear things like, "Oregon shouldn't have even been there, so it's not a true win." "Alabama could have beat them if, (fill in the blank)"

Let me remind you the Pharisees followed Jesus all over trying to prove him wrong. They watched and waited for him to mess up. Jesus did miracles over and over again. The few that we read about in the New Testament, was a very small percentage of all he did. The Pharisees saw most of them. They criticized Jesus for healing on the Sabbath. They didn't deny the fact the healing took place, but they still didn't believe. So "Seeing isn't Believing."

Faith is the evidence of things unseen. When we believe before we see, God honors that and great things follow. There can be times you need help and it's OK to ask God for a sign or confirmation. Demanding as if God worked for you, is quite different than a heart felt request for help in your unbelief.

God doesn't work for us. His will is more important than our will. Our will can match God's will. This happens when we seek his face and will first. As we grow closer to God through Prayer, Bible, and Quiet time. When God's love fills us and we begin to love like him, we start to desire good for others. This is when our will becomes more like God's.

He wants good for all his family. So should we.

Day 85

Matthew 16:6 – Beware and Pray

6 "Watch out!" Jesus warned them. "Beware of the yeast of the Pharisees and Sadducees." NLT

The first thing to remember is the fact Yeast is a representation of Sin. The Passover meal had flat bread, or crackers without yeast. "Sinless bread."

Jesus is telling us to avoid sin. Not just in our own lives, but also in the church leadership. We do not need to be over critical, Pastors are human too. However patterns of unfaithfulness, how they treat others, pride, and disseat, are a few things that may cause you to leave a church or to avoid them personally. This is something that needs to be done in prayer. God may have a need for you there. Let the Holy Spirit guide you. Most likely it's not the pastor that would apply. Most of you are in a very good church. However, it's the person at work that is overly religious that gets on your nerves. They seem to be bold with their faith so you hate to think bad things, and over look patterns.

Questions: Are they using their faith for personal gain? Are they using their faith to prove they are better than others? Are they using their faith in ways that lifts them up but not Jesus? If yes, then you need to protect yourself. Staying in the Word (bible) first off, helps us see through the false front or lies. You also need to pray for them to understand how they are hurting people and for them to see there motives. They very well, may think they are helping. Pray for how you should handle it. What to say and when to avoid, can only be determined by God. I can't help you with the specifics.

The Holy Spirit is the best guide and giver of wisdom. GO to God and get the help you need to deal with the Sadducees in your life. In most cases you just need to know their motives and not be influenced by them. Beware, I think is a warning to know the people around you and don't listen to the garbage. Filter it out with the Word.

Day 86

Matthew 16:7 – Understanding

"Here's your Sign."

They didn't get it. Like someone walking into the room looking at the big sheet cake on the table and all the decorations and says, "Is there a party or something going on?" We often find ourselves in situations that we just want to say, "Duh!" Ok, some of us do say it. But I am off subject.

Understanding spiritual things can seem very simple and other times, we get caught in a conversation in which we feel like they are in a different world. The Pharisees knew the scripture better than the average person. They had memorized lots of scriptures. They spent hours and hours at church. They were the perfect Religious example. Church regulars, with an extensive knowledge of the scriptures, some would say they would love to be like them. They would be wrong. With all the hours and the knowledge, they still had no idea what Jesus was talking about. This was not an isolated case. The Pharisees were always in the dark. Jesus talked in plain speech and word pictures. Uneducated fishermen and farmers understood.

My point is this. While studying the Word is very important, it is not enough. It is our relationship with Jesus that makes the true difference. We must have turned our life over to Jesus through repentance.

The great thing is when we look to Jesus, we can have great understanding. Listening to the Spirit as you read the Bible, leads to understanding. If we read it for our own gain, with no interest in getting to know Jesus, the Holy Spirit who is the source of all understanding will hide the truth from us. Motives are important. Having the desire to get to know Jesus is the start to understanding. Once we have this desire, then we can find understanding when we read. Opening up to the Holy Spirit takes humility and leads to amazing moments.

Our level of knowledge and years of being a believer is not a limitation to God talking to us and you being able to understand it. Miracles can happen to you and through you. Seek Jesus first, and amazing things will follow.

In addition to this, you cannot only understand but you can do. Do not live under the weight of condemnation. Feeling you are stupid is a feeling with no merit. If you don't move into action, because you feel like others are better, you miss out on your own personal blessing. Don't miss out. You are every bit as capable and every bit as loved by God as anyone else.

Day 87

Matthew 16:15 – Who is Jesus

15 "Then he asked them, "But who do you say I am?" NLT

This follows Jesus talking to the disciples about who people thought he was. The point is that it is not a matter of what others think about Jesus. It only matters what you think. I can't repent for you. I can forgive you in my own limited capacity, but my forgiveness is not enough to give you eternal life. Eternal life is a gift from GOD. I cannot purchase it for you, and you cannot get it from me.

It is up to all of us to call on Jesus for ourselves.

Who do you say that he is?

I say that he is the Son of God, creator of everything. The Son of Man, born into flesh, living a sinless life. I believe he died, and ROSE again. He defeated death and sin. I believe he is the one who purchased my place in heaven with his own blood. He is my savior and the one who will come back and retrieve those who have called on him. He will be our king for all time and will welcome us to heaven when we die.

My belief in him includes a trust that he will forgive and save me. He is also the only way to get to heaven and I have put my faith in his grace and no longer depend on my own ability.

Again – **Who do you say that he is?**

Day 88

Matthew 16:17 – Understanding Revealed

17 Jesus replied, "You are blessed, Simon son of John, because my Father in heaven has revealed this to you. You did not learn this from any human being. NLT

Peter has just told Jesus who he was, and Peter was correct. Here Jesus is letting Peter and the disciples know that knowledge of the godly things comes from the Father through the Holy Spirit. The Truth of Jesus is reveled to us through the Holy Spirit. Not from each other. Our Faith comes from the Reading of the Bible. The understanding of the Bible comes from God. His ways and wisdom are beyond our understanding.

The great thing is, when we seek him we will find him, and find understanding. We can have all the understanding we need every time we need. Of course it will come as we need it, not always as we want it. But when the understanding comes, it comes at the right time. For me it often comes, not for me, but for me to share with some one that needs confirmation of what the Holy Spirit is telling them. So understand this, our understanding isn't always for just us, it is often for some one else as well.

God has understanding and wisdom for you. Keep looking for it. The bible is the best place to look.

Day 89

Matthew 16:23 – Jesus is in Control

Four verses after Jesus praised Peter and declared him the Rock, he is calling him Satan. My how the mighty have fallen.

Good lesson; **don't get a big head**. If you are being praised, watch your step, you may be right around the corner from a big mess up. Which is OK; Peter did it. We are human. We are going to make mistakes. Humility will help take you through these times, if not be caused by them. Humility is also a great way to avoid mistakes. So we are ALL able to fall short of perfection. Jesus alone is our perfection, so relax. We are forgivable.

The rebuke of Peter was not for an act. It was for doing what many of us would think was a good thing. In man's eyes he didn't say anything wrong. What did he say? He told Jesus he wasn't going to let anyone hurt or kill him. Very heroic. He was coming to Jesus' defense. What could be wrong with that? He loved Jesus.

First Jesus doesn't need our help.

Secondly, Peter was trying to stop the very reason Jesus came to earth. Jesus had to die. He was not going to be captured and murdered. He was going give himself up to be sacrificed. The sin wasn't in the desire to help. The sin was in trying to stop the **Will of God.**

There are bad things that happen. There are also things that happen that aren't bad, just not what we would like. Before we speak out against it; we need to make sure it isn't God's will for it to happen. Never forget. Jesus is in FULL Control. Don't stand in the way. Even if it seems bad, Jesus will make something great out of it. If we let him.

Today we are going to let him have his way, and pray for wisdom to follow and do as we need to.

Day 90

Matthew 17:1-7 – After Death

Breaking from the 'Written in Red' track I've been on, I want to take a look at what is going on here. What I see are two men of faith that have not finished serving God. Here Elijah and Moses have returned. They talked with Jesus. I don't know if Jesus needed their help, or if they were there for us to see them. There is life after death. Not only life after death, there is service after death. We aren't just going to be in robes, standing in one spot for eternity.

Heaven is actually temporary as well as our time on earth. We return with Jesus in the second coming. This is when Jesus returns for his 1000 year reign. Big battle, Satan is defeated, and a New Jerusalem comes down. I believe we will be back on earth when it is reborn and we will inhabit it forever after that.

What we go through here on earth helps us and others on this part of the journey. But I believe it also develops skills for our eternal journey. I don't know what kind of obstacles we'll have after that, but I think we'll have something to do.

The second thing that stood out for the first time, the two men God used. We know Elijah didn't die. He could have easily come back for a visit, but Moses did die. He was buried. The fact that he returned as well, shows us we have a future even after death.

We see that Jesus had an inner circle. Moses and Elijah were great men of faith and close to God also. Does that mean we are outcasts? We are measured by our faith. We can each pursue faith. We can get closer to God. We can be great men and women of faith. Even though there were nine disciples left behind, each of them was used by God in very special ways. Then the next circle out was the five hundred believers who gathered after the resurrection. So no matter which circle you are in, Jesus' Love is real. His desire is to use you in miraculous ways. He wants nothing more than to get closer to you.

Seek Wisdom, Faith, and Jesus. You will find, him an all that goes with him. Don't settle on the outer circle, you can work your way in.

Day 91

Matthew 17:17-20 – Faith, Prayer, & Fasting

Jesus is a little frustrated. I think it has a lot to do with the fact the end was coming soon, and he only had a short time to teach them everything he needed to. Even after two years, they just weren't getting it.

It's not about the words.
It's not about who you know.
It's not about the side you are on.

It is all about FAITH and connecting it with the power of the Holy Spirit.

We connect to it through Prayer. Prayer is more intense when it is coupled with Fasting.

As Jesus says, it doesn't take a lot of Faith, which means we **all** have enough. If it is applied, that is.

The disciples tried to cast the demons out, just like Jesus did. They did everything just as he did. But they missed one important thing. Jesus was in Pray all the time. He fasted, and found quiet time to talk to God his father.

There are no step by step instructions for miracles. God mixes it up. Only the Holy Spirit knows how it will work next. Rituals do not work. Religious acts do not work.

Prayer, Fasting, and Faith. (Can't have faith without the word) The Bible.

Day 92

Matthew 17:20 – Don't Doubt God

    Faith without doubt, is the only true Faith. Doubt is the opposite of faith. We often speak of sports teams with an assurance they will win the championship. But do we believe enough to bet everything we have on a team at the beginning of the season? If we did it wouldn't be faith it would be crazy. What a good fan does is verbalize the hope all season long, staying positive, despite a few losses early on.

    If I knew the future I would be able to bet my 401K on a single game. I could put everything on the line and wouldn't have to sweet it out until the final buzzer.

    When I pray, do I put my entire life on the line? Do I give it everything I have? When I pray, do I have apprehension over what might go wrong in the words I use or whether God wants to do anything? Even while we pray do we think about the "What if's"

    I haven't prayed for healing for someone, with the intensity that I would if I truly knew the future. We know (or should know) that all things work for the good of those who love the Lord. We know that Jesus loves us and Answers our prayers. We know that. But we question it, at least a little.

    Spending time in prayer, and I mean more than 3 minutes a day. I mean real time of prayer. We need to be willing to fast. These things will draw us closer to God and more sensitive to the Holy Spirit. Following his lead and timing, enhances our ability to be used. The most important thing to remember in all this is; it is still God doing the miracle.

    Keep this in mind, we don't have to doubt ourselves for a second. It's not us doing the healing or other miracles. It's God. The only thing we have to believe is that God can do it and will do it.

Let God be God.

Day 93

Matthew 18:2-4 – Like a Child

4 So anyone who becomes as humble as this little child is the greatest in the Kingdom of Heaven. NLT

We need to be like a child. We need to be able to believe the unbelievable. Things like believing a coin can come out of your ear. Believe that the Easter Bunny paints and delivers eggs. Believe the tooth fairy actually wants your teeth so much he will pay for them. How about believing Jesus will heal your boo boo. They even believe Noah fit all the animals into the ark.

It seems like I lumped fantasy with the Bible. The truth is, readers will be unclear on the animals or whether Jesus does heal boo boos. So much of life can be explained away, that faith isn't needed to live. But the lack of faith definitely leads to death.

Faith like a child means we believe what Jesus tells us without over analyzing it. Without questioning whether it is possible. Every thing **IS** possible. EVERYTHING!

Adults over analyze everything. Adults only believe what they see, and don't believe half of what they do.

Do you believe?

Do you believe Jesus wants what's best for you?

Do you believe miracles can happen to you and through you?

Do you believe Jesus is alive and listening to your prayers?

Do you believe Jesus Loves you?

Day 94

Matthew 18:7 – Don't Hold Back

7 "What sorrow awaits the world, because it tempts people to sin. Temptations are inevitable, but what sorrow awaits the person who does the tempting. NLT

This is about talking people into doing things that will make you happy. The tempting is most likely wrapped in a lie. How else would someone fall for a bad idea?

Lying to get someone to do your will, leads to bad things. The key to the last sentence is, Your WILL. When we put our will above God's Will, bad things happen, to you and to those around you.

Not telling someone about Jesus, because it might change them into someone else. Fear of change. Fear that your relationship will be different. It will. SO don't be afraid.

The fact is, the change is better that no change.
The change is Jesus, and how can that be bad?

Jesus is here to make everything better. Better is often different, otherwise it would just be the same. SO if you want life to be better, it's going to take change. Change when done with the leading of the Holy Spirit, is always good. Sorry, its always great.

DO not settle for the same and do NOT cause others to stay the same.

In others words, **don't** hold some one else back, and don't hold yourself back.

DON'T HOLD BACK!

Day 95

Matthew 18:12 – God Wants You

*12 "If a man has a hundred sheep and one of them wanders away, what will he do? Won't he leave the ninety-nine others on the hills and go out to search for the one that is lost?
13 And if he finds it, I tell you the truth, he will rejoice over it more than over the ninety-nine that didn't wander away!
14 In the same way, it is not my heavenly Father's will that even one of these little ones should perish. NLT*

I always thought this wasn't a very good example. I'm no shepherd, but wouldn't it be irresponsible to leave the other 99? What if they run away or split up while you're gone.

Over analyzing Jesus' words can keep us from the truth of his message. The point is no matter how much we have if we loose something, that's all that's on our mind.

Coin, Pen, CD, or anything that we know is missing; we dig and search until we find it or go crazy looking for it. How about a missing remote? I think God looks for us like we look for the missing remote.

It is that same way with God and us. He drives himself crazy thinking about the fact any of us are going to hell. His love for us is unending. He will send us messages over and over again. Many of us can agree with this and can share examples of how many hints and chances the Holy Spirit gave us before we finally gave in and repented. His mercy is fantastic, giving us multiple chances before giving up on us.

If you feel like you have wandered off, don't work yourself up over it. God wants you back in a big way. He is looking for you and calling for you right now. You may have even heard him, but fear has you holding back. Stop holding back, all you have to fear is his conditional love and peace.

God Wants You!

Day 96

Matthew 18:19-20 – Jesus is Here

This does not mean we can get anything against God's will. It does mean if we gather together and seeks God's will and pray together over it he will give it. When we gather together with fellow believers, He is there amongst us. When we gather together even if it is just one on one, we have Jesus with us to help us through any problem we have.

We often mistake this verse, as a way to get a physical wish. God is not a Genie in a Bottle. What can or should we be asking for? Guidance, Wisdom, Healing, Peace, Help, and Vision.

What have you been asking for? Is it what you need or only what you want? Our wants don't always benefit us or the Church Family. God's will, as I mentioned earlier, is for the spread of his Love, and for the entire family to be healed and helped.

I don't want my wants to interfere with God's plan and will. I want my wants to benefit my brothers in Christ. I want my desires to be for Jesus and sharing his Love.

When I gather with my friends and wife, I need to remember that Jesus is with us, and seize that opportunity and not take it for granted. Jesus is here to answer or prayers, just as he has promised. So do we pray and seek wisdom or do we complain and bring each other down.

I know what I do. But I'll try to do better next time.

Sometimes I think complaining is so much more fun, but I am wrong. Actually Answered Prayer is way better on any given day. Take advantage of every time you are with believers. Jesus is there. Still have fun, but keep your heart open to the leading of the Spirit.

He is Here!

Day 97

Matthew 18:22 – Forgive and Remember

22"No, not seven times," Jesus replied, "but seventy times seven!

Forgiveness; It is something we all think we deserve, but have a hard time giving it. This is the verse that points out that we aren't to just forgive them once, but as many times as it takes. Jesus died for our forgiveness. God gives his mercy every morning for as long as we live. He forgives us every time we ask. So shouldn't we do the same?

It is a fact; grudges are easy, while forgiveness is tough.

I think that most of the time we don't want to forgive. When we are hurt by someone, we think about it all the time. The more we think about it, the more hurt we get. It continues in a vicious circle. Even if we try to forgive, the memory of it comes back. Because we are not able to forget about it, we don't want to forgive. It's easy to think, forgiving will be alright when it stops bothering us. Problem is, it won't stop bothering us until we can forget about it.

Then just when we think we've forgotten about it, we see them at the store or across the room, and it all comes rushing back.

To forgive, we first need to want to.
Then we need the Holy Spirit to help.
Then we need to pray over it every time we think about it.

Jesus forgives us because he wants to.

I want to forgive even while I remember. Because then I can remember the grace that covers me, and how it flowed through me onto someone else.

So Forgive and Remember

Day 98

Matthew 19:4 – Know the Truth

4 "Haven't you read the Scriptures?" Jesus replied. NLT

Before the argument started, Jesus simply asked if they have read the Bible. This is before there was a New Testament and before it was called a Bible. Never the less, it was still God's Word. It is the way we get our wisdom. It is our source.

Here the Pharisees are trying to trap Jesus. Today, some may try to use the scriptures to trick you or lead you astray. Many will twist the scriptures to make it mean what they want it to. They may twist it to justify an action or feeling they may have. Perhaps you have done the same.

Before you use the scriptures be sure to read it.

Once you know it, you will hear it missed used all the time. So many people try to use the scripture but don't read it, so they either use it out of context or just plan misuse it.

Example; "God helps those who help themselves."
Believe it or not, this is NOT in the Bible.

"Eye for an Eye" used as an excuse for revenge, but this one scripture, that Jesus corrected. It's use several times while he was here on earth. If you know God's Word, then you will know that Jesus does not condone revenge, in fact he tells us not to do it. Jesus said to "Love your Enemy"

Read the Bible. Get to know it. Learn the Truth.
Do not be deceived.
If you don't want to misrepresent Jesus Read it.
If you don't want to be mislead, Read it.

Day 99

Matthew 19:8 – The Perfect Life

God hates divorce. This is not to make people who have already been divorced feel bad. Forgiveness is still just as real for divorced people as anyone else. It does not eliminate your chances for heaven.

The point for today is for our younger readers. Marriage is very serious to God. It should be serious to all of us. It is not a fun life to be stuck in a relationship that you knew was wrong to begin with.

Picking the right mate the first time is a great thing. Lisa and I have been together for 20 years, most of them have been great. In all 20 years, I have never doubted that she was the one I was supposed to marry. What Joy to have the perfect fit for me. It is so hard to see others struggle.

As followers of Jesus, we have the advantage of the Holy Spirit. There is no reason not to marry the right one the first time. It's when we try to handle it ourselves. Never rush it. Never settle for the one you know, thinking there can't be anyone better.

Never settle.

God has the perfect one for you. If it is in his plan for you to be single, then the best life you can have is to be single and in God's will. The best life, even during struggles is a life in God's will. You can have the perfect life for you. It is important not to let the wrong person mess up the perfect life. Be patient, pray about your spouse to be. Listen to the Spirit and you will do well.

Marriage is the biggest thing we do. Don't go into it without God's leading and direction. We pray for help in everything else. By the way this includes dating. Dating the wrong person, can keep you from moving in the direction God is leading you in.

The perfect life is in Jesus and in his plan.

Day 100

Matthew 19:14 – The Child of Faith

It would be no surprise to most of you, that I would include this verse. After all, besides playing on the computer talking to y'all, my main ministry is Children.

As most people, who serve in ministry, I think I have the best. Difference is, Jesus agrees with me. Just kidding, every ministry is equally important. We must all do the one God has called us to.

I believe Jesus points this out to us, because it is so easy to over look them. Too often we see children as little creatures without a clue of what real life is all about. This is true, but God isn't looking for people who know a lot or have the whole world figured out. He does not need highly developed brains to solve all the problems of the world. What God needs, or should I say wants, is people of FAITH.

Children display greater faith than 98% of all adults on a daily basis. Do they doubt anything when they are small? Like Santa being able to go around the whole world in a single night or a kiss will make a boo-boo better. This is unshaken faith.

Our unshaken faith needs to be that Jesus is God. That he did die and rise again, and does love us. I can ask any of my kids at church, if they think Jesus loves them, every one of them would say yes. Ask the same question to 20 adults, and the results would vary with every person.

Do you believe that Jesus loves you?
DO you believe with even a little doubt, that Jesus wants you to succeed?
Do you believe Jesus will help you through any thing?

Can you answer these questions honestly? I hope I can say yes, but sometimes I struggle with number 3.

Day 101

Matthew 19:21 – Not Good Enough

You must know this comes after the people were asking questions about how to get to heaven, and which commandments are the most important. Jesus saw through them and knew it wasn't a question for true direction. They were asking only so they could brag about how good they are. In verse 17 Jesus says only one is Good, and that is God.

So Jesus is adding requirements until they are shut up by the final instruction. Sell it all. He knew they were not interested in being better, or perfect. They were already convinced they were perfect. But Jesus tells them to give it all away. He knows exactly what we are not willing to give up. I'm not going to get into giving up stuff to get closer to God today. I want you to understand, that this rabbit trail for these men, was not a list for entry to Heaven for all of us. He was simply showing that these men weren't as good as they thought they were.

Humility is what they didn't have. We all need to be Humble. For Heaven is a result of our Humility and Repentance.

If you want to be perfect, be like Jesus. He gave up everything including life. No matter what we do we will always come up short of Jesus' greatness.

He is always twenty steps ahead of us. So just give up and follow his lead. Do what you know he is telling you to do. He told several to sell everything, but not everyone. His direction is specific to each of us. Do not go and do things just because you read it or a friend has done it. Do what the Lord is leading you to do. We do it to get closer to God and to increase our ability to be used by God. Heaven is through Grace and Repentance. We do Good out of Love, not out of Fear, or to get something for our good deed.

Do it all in Love

Day 102

Matthew 20:13 – God isn't Fair, Thank God.

Jesus just told the story of the Vineyard Owner. He hired groups of men through out the day. At the end of the day he paid all the men the same amount of money. Today we'd call it a Salary. Because they weren't paid by the hour it seemed very unfair. The men that went to work first, worked more hours for the money. So if it is broken down by the hour, they got paid less, in theory.

But they all got paid the same.

We can get caught up in over thinking our own situation. Whether it is over money or position, we can turn even good things into something to complain about. This is not just about work or school but also about church ministry. Is it fair?

Is life ever fair when we measure it by the hour, or worse, by our own standards? Not really, if we look at it through our own eyes alone. But lets look at it through Jesus' eyes.

As Jesus hung on the cross with blood running down his face, the blood and sweat stung as it entered his eyes. He still opened his eyes and looked out on the crowd that was physically killing him. He looked at both those who were active and inactive in the process. Jesus also looked at all the men and women through out time, whose sin had driven the nails in his hands. This includes all of us who failed and have sinned. He looked through his own sinless blood and forgave all of us. It is forgiveness for anyone who would ask for that forgiveness. Is that fair? No. No matter how you look at it.

Is it fair that many of us have served God for 30 years, and Jesus turned to the thief, forgave him and let him go to heaven without ever getting a chance to serve him? He didn't serve in the choir, greeting team, nursery, or prison ministry.

The gift is God's to give. He is the only one who paid for it. He gives it as he pleases. It should please us to get the gift of eternal life, as well as anyone else we can bring along. Black, White, Rich, Poor, Tattooed, Drug addicts, or just a plain bad person, it doesn't matter. Jesus Forgives them all.

Humility and Repentance.

It is the one thing that levels the playing field. None of us are worthy of such a sacrifice or gift. But here it is. Jesus offers it freely.

Do not feel you are not worthy enough, or that someone else is less deserving. Our past is not the issue, when the Payment comes we need to be thankful for being a part of God's plan and work, and everything else that goes with it.

I am so thankful God isn't fair.

Personalities vary but Jesus can use us all.

I wish the Bible told us more about the disciples. I am one who would love to know what all their personalities were. With twelve men, there was every personality possible. Whiners, complainers, morning people, night owls, one that was way too happy about everything that was going on, one who doubted everything, (Thomas) one who never actually listened to Jesus, because he was too busy figuring out how Jesus should be doing things. (Judas), lazy ones, busy bodies, and those that listened and knew all the answers, and there had to be a goodie two shoes as well, and Jesus hand picked everyone of them. They were transformed into incredible men of God. Eleven of them are sitting with Jesus as heroes today.

Day 103

Matthew 20:18-19 – We have what it takes

I find it interesting that Jesus refers to himself in the 3rd person. But that's not the point for today. I have talked about Jesus being the Son of Man, before. Here's a refresher. We are all sons or daughters of man. But Jesus is "THE Son of Man". Jesus is also the Son of God. This means he is both God and Man.

Here he is pointing out that his days as the Son of Man are coming to an end. He tells the 12 exactly what is about to happen. I'm sure they didn't believe him, at least not yet. Remember they didn't believe Lazarus would live again. They didn't believe Jesus could feed 4000, even though they had seen him feed 5000. They had very short memories. Now here Jesus is giving the layout of his death.

This is a turning point. They would never forget this one. Remember they didn't have the advantage that we do today. Yes, they had Jesus face to face. But that didn't seem to be enough. They didn't have the Bible to carry with them. That's not it either. They didn't have the **Holy Spirit**. The disciples don't get the Holy Spirit until Pentecost, in Acts 2.

You can see the transformation that takes place after Pentecost. These men were unstoppable.
We need the Word.
We need Jesus.
We need Forgiveness.
We need a relationship.
But all this isn't enough. We need the Holy Spirit.

That's the whole reason Jesus had to go, so the Spirit could come. Now we have God with us all the time. The Holy Spirit pulls all our faith, the Word we've read, and our experience together into a usable force; a force that is powered by God himself.

So remember we have what they did, The Holy Spirit.

Day 104

Matthew 20:20-21 – What's your Answer

I will use this out of context to a certain extent. But I think in this case it will be alright. If Jesus was over to the house, what would you fix him for dinner? I got side tracked. But it's still a good question. Jameson would want to make home made pizza. I would serve Oreos and Cherry Coke, if he was just stopping by for a minute. For Dinner, I would have to make a Costco run. Smoke Salmon and Horseradish cheese on crackers. I would then pan frie some tilapia. So the table is set you are chilling with Jesus. He turns to you and asks you the same question as in Verse 21. What would your reply be?

What is your desire? What is your wish? What do you want to do with your life? Ask yourself these questions without disqualifying them. Do you find yourself ignoring your dreams because of the following?

You may feel Too old, No funds, not enough Talent, don't know how, no time, or just can't do it. We are able to come up with so many reasons why God can't use us, or won't do anything for us. How can we limit God? God has no limits. He has no weaknesses. We limit God through our lack of faith. Will our answer be "A second slice of Pie." when we are face to face with the creator of the universe, will the answer be a complete cop out.

Sunday night I prayed with a man who was about to start a 33 year ministry dream. Noah had to wait until he was well past a hundred. Peter was an uneducated fisherman. David was the smallest of his brothers and overlooked. I'm dyslexic and I failed reading and had to repeat the fifth grade.

When Jesus asks you what you wish, be as bold as James and John. They asked to sit at his side as he ruled the world. They got their wish. It cost a price. James was one of the first to be killed.

So what's your answer?

Day 105

Matthew 21:1&2 – Just Go

Here is the day of Jesus' triumphant entry into Jerusalem. We see Jesus' instructions. Here we have two disciples on their way back with a Donkey, just like Jesus had described. I can just see them walking back. Should they take turns riding it? No, it is for Jesus. Does it matter? They probably didn't ride it, but more because they couldn't agree on who should go first, than reverence to Jesus. But then they couldn't stop talking about how they actually found the Donkey. And the fact the man just let them take it without much of an explanation.

The arguing that would take place on the way back was probably filled with laughter. "I never doubted Jesus for a minute." and "Just like all the miracles before." each trying to prove they had more faith than the other.

What about the trip to get the Donkey? They probably talked about what they were going to do when they didn't find a donkey. "We can't go back empty handed." "I think there will be a donkey. But the owner is never going to let us go with that little excuse. Don't worry, I'll think of something."

I can see the owner of the donkey stopping them, "Hey, what are you doing with my donkey?" Then the Disciple that was so sure about his ability to handle the situation better than Jesus, freezes up and stutters, "The Lord needs it." he chokes and says it just as Jesus told him to.

We don't have to go with perfect faith, we just need to go. I don't know all the details of the donkey project, but even if they had doubt they still went. Even if they stumbled through it, they still did it. Not only did they move forward, they were successful in their trip.

All of us can be a success. Just follow Jesus' instructions.

His instructions are in his Word, (Bible)

Day 106

Matthew 21:13 – What's the Motive

This is not an attack on churches that have a book store, or a corner that sells CD's and Books. As everything Jesus has cut down before. It is about focus. Is Jesus still the focus? Are the books being sold there to help the body get closer to God? If it becomes, just a source of revenue for the church, then maybe it's not lining up with God's wishes. I was in a Christian book store yesterday. They were selling biographies. Many of them were good. But there were a couple of books by very famous people. They probably sold very well, but they were not Christians. Even though I did not read them, I can pretty much guarantee, as awesome as the book may be, it won't point you to God.

I am fine with anyone buying the book. But I would not support selling them at my church, especially any book that doesn't point to God. Jesus always needs to be the focal point. We sell CDs at the churches we sing at. We give more away than is financially smart. But we sing as a ministry. We desire to bless people and do it in a manor that brings honor to God, not just ourselves.

There are many more reasons for bringing dishonor to the church, than just selling. In the case above, they weren't just selling books; they were cheating people, scamming people and much more.

So I guess the point is this:
What's the motivation in anything we do; **Self or God?** This applies to every aspect of church, from singing for self glory, to joining a committee so you can run it the way you think it needs to be run. When serving God is overshadowed by serving self or agenda, then it becomes a den of thieves. So it's more than just money.

It is all about Jesus over us.

Day 107

Matthew 21:21 – By Faith

FAITH: Jesus points this out over and over again. It took Jesus dying and coming back to life for his disciples to catch on. Actually it took the Holy Spirit. I think most of us are just as hard headed. The lack of faith is so overwhelming, that we can't believe anything we can't see. Or worse, we don't believe good things can happen to us or for us. Insecurity is built on a lie from Hell that God doesn't really care. This is a LIE.

Insecurity like Worry is the opposite of Faith. Worry is the FEAR of something bad is about to happen, while Insecurity is the FEAR that nothing good will happen. It is basically the same thing. The cause of both is belief in this LIE.

Here are some samples of the lies:
Not worthy of anything good, Not good enough. Don't deserve it.
God doesn't love me, even if he loves the whole rest of the world.
God never really forgave me. I'm to bad to be loved.
I have nothing God would want..

It is all about our faith. If we have faith in God to bring us a good mate, he will bring them. If we have faith that God has the perfect Job for us, He will supply it. Faith needs to be not just a prayer of request as the verses may suggest. It is an action word. Filling out the application and going to an interview is acting on faith. It is very rare, you will get a call out of the blue with no effort by you, to get an interview or offer letter. The perfect bride must be asked, and must accept. It may take a phone call. It may take a dinner reservation. It will take some effort. But what makes those efforts a miracle, is the Faith we have in God's Love and Grace. We need to have Faith that God does want what's best for us. When the Holy Spirit leads, it's going to be good, so follow and do whatever he leads you to do.

BY FAITH.

Day 108

Matthew 21:31-32 – Not About Our Past

This is good news. Not for those who are too righteous to repent or those who are too smart for Jesus. It is good news for those of us who have a history of bad behavior. Those of us who understand the level of grace it takes to cover our sins.

It is incredible news for us that need Jesus because no one else will forgive us. How about those of us who have had a hard time looking in the mirror, because of self-discus?

Jesus bled for our sins, no matter how bad it is, and no matter how colorful our past.

It's not about our past or twenty minutes ago. It's all about our attitude towards Jesus and his gift of forgiveness.

If we are humble and sorry, all it takes is vocalizing our repentance and bam, our sins are gone.

When I say gone, I mean we can go freely and without shame, to God.

We ARE part of his Family.
We ARE Forgiven.
We ARE set Free.
We ARE fully Loved.
We ARE Royalty.

Day 109

Matthew 22:1-10 – Obligation or Love

Jesus is not looking to force anyone into a relationship with him. Our Free will is a dangerous thing for all of us. It is at the same time a big blessing. God wants us to come to him freely and under our own will. Linking our Will with his Will must come from us.

Here the King invited the good choice people of the kingdom to the party. But they didn't come. So he invited the poor. He realized the party would be much better with people that wanted to be there, instead of people that were only there out of obligation.

Are we doing church out of obligation?
Are we merely pretending to love out of obligation?

Obligation is not a commandment. Actually it is the opposite of his commandments. As Jesus explains; It is good not to commit murder, but if we are filled with hate and wish they were dead it is the same thing in God's eyes. God looks at our heart not just our actions.

Our actions usually follow our heart, but not always. The Bible tells us that our mouth is the true sign of our heart.

When it comes to giving, God tells us to be a cheerful giver. He doesn't say give anyway. As a deacon in the church who has the responsibility of the finances, I'll say give anyway. Give first and work on the attitude about it later. But see the pattern Jesus is setting up, give because you want to, Love with a true heart of love. Hate is just as bad as physical harm. He only wants those who truly love him in heaven. If you don't feel like you love him enough, don't worry. He can help you with that.

Like I said at the beginning; It was the people that wanted to come that were invited. Once we are at the party (born again) the Holy Spirit can help with the rest.

Day 110

Matthew 22:29 – The Source

This is after the Sadducees try to trick Jesus again, they just don't know when to quit. The scriptures are about whether we will be married after we die. But verse 29 really sticks out. I can't tell you how many times I have listened to someone who thinks they know the scriptures and have based there religious beliefs on a half truth. The conversation will most likely include. "I don't believe in organized religion." or "My religion is personal so I don't go to a church, it's filled with hypocrites" Bottom line is they don't go to any church and it doesn't take long to figure out they don't or have never read the bible. Their whole knowledge of the scriptures is based on a few hymns and what they've heard on TV.

There have been times I have been confused, and down right wrong. The cure for it has always been reading the word. I have always relied more on the Bible for my knowledge and wisdom, than any other books. As a result, I have remained fairly grounded; Grounded on the solid foundation of God's Word.

This is the source of Faith, Wisdom, and Guidance.

If you are confused, GO TO THE BIBLE.
If you aren't sure what you believe, GO TO THE BIBLE.
If you just don't know, GO TO THE BIBLE.
If you have a hard time following the pastor's message, GO TO THE BIBLE. You will either find understanding, or realize your pastor is wrong. Either way, you will know God's view.

To understand God and his Kingdom, you must go to the scripture. To fully understand the Power of God, we must read the word. If going to church was enough the world would be a much better place. But the churches are filled with people that do not know the scriptures for the y do not read the scriptures. They also do not understand the Power of God; therefore they do not know how to tap into that Power.

You have the power at your reach, reach out and read it.

Day 111

Matthew 22:31 – Life With Jesus

I don't think there is much to say on this one. It is very clear what Jesus is saying. Death of the physical body is not the end. We live on.

Death of the Body, allows our soul and spirit to be with Jesus. We cannot be with Jesus in the Physical until our bodies are healed 100%. That doesn't happen until we have the physical death.

At this point we join Jesus if and only if we have repented before this death comes.

We must be born again, before the 1st death. If we don't repent then the physical death that have again doesn't end our Spirits life, but the life after death is not with God. The absence of God is hell, and ends up in a place void of Love.

God is Love. SO without God, we are without Love.

Even on our worst day, the Holy Spirit is close by with love.
Even if we don't always feel it, the world is filled with love.
Even those who are not saved or a Christian, have the capacity to love. Anyone can Love children or wife.

Death without repentance ends in life with no Love of any kind.

Good news:
If we turn to Jesus, our 1st death leads to life with Jesus. That is awesome.

Day 112

Matthew 24:4-8 – The Only Way

Being misled continues even today, with more still to come. What we see is nothing new. It has happened over and over. The newest re-used lie is that there isn't a Hell. The persecution from those who claim to be out to protect others is highly visible. Be politically correct and don't say anything against someone else's belief. If you don't give into others beliefs you are in danger of persecution.

The media is not only out to destroy our voice, it is also an amazing way to reach more people than can be imagined without. But it places those on TV at a disadvantage. They are under a microscope, and to keep the following of thousands and rating, and air time, compromises are being made. They find themselves saying things they don't even believe, some from ignorance and others from fear. Some are getting backed into a corner and instead of following the Spirit, they compromise.

So when asked point blank "Do you believe that Jesus is the only way to heaven?" it's a trap much like the Pharisees trying to trap Jesus. If they have the sense to say yes, the follow-up question is; "So all the Japanese who didn't know Jesus, went to Hell?"

Could you answer the question? I wouldn't want to on TV. But these men have placed themselves on TV as representatives of Jesus. Where much is given, much is required. The true answer unfortunately is Yes If they didn't know Jesus. This is a horrible truth. And all the more reason we need to work harder to spread the gospel so everyone can have the chance to accept Jesus. How about loved ones that are sick and don't want to even talk about church or Jesus. We can't wish them into Heaven.

This is a tough subject. If we compromise on this one we are saying Jesus' Blood was not needed.

Support Verses: John 14:6, John 10:9, & Romans 5:2

Day 113

Matthew 25:31 – No Judgment

There will be a pre-separation; meaning before the judgment. God is going to separate us out from those who do not turn to Jesus prior to death. Those of us who have accepted Jesus and his Grace and Forgiveness, will be lead into the kingdom.

Those who don't have the forgiveness of Christ, will be held for Judgment.

See there is no fear in Christ Jesus. What's the worst that can happen? We die and go to Jesus? That is alright with me. There is no condemnation in Jesus.

John 3:18 "There is no judgment against anyone who believes in him. But anyone who does not believe in him has already been judged for not believing in God's one and only Son." NLT

When we turn to Jesus and humble ourselves in repentance. Asking him for forgiveness, we are washed by his blood that was shed as the penalty for our sins. The debt for our sin has been paid by Jesus. Now we can ask for the forgiveness, and actually receive it. This forgiveness is forever. When we die we don't have to claim the blood again, he will be waiting for us.

I believe we have full free will, so we can always give back the gift of eternal life, but it can never be lost or taken away. The devil would love to take it from you, but he can't. All he can do is lie to you and try to talk you into giving it up. Most never do, but he continues to try.

Life is simple from here on out. **Don't listen to the lie, Keep your eyes on Jesus** and look forward to eternal life with Jesus. If you don't have it, ask for it. Take hold and never let go.

Day 114

Matthew 25:44 & 45 – Something for Nothing

It is good to see exactly what Jesus is saying. He is so often misquoted. There is no mistake what he is telling us to do here.

If we want to honor him, we must help the needy. I am blessed to be part of a church that believes in this. We have a program called Manna that gives food and clothing out to those who needs help. They also give counseling and a chance to hear the gospel.

I am not telling you to give money to the guy on the corner with a sign. But look for an organization you can help with your time or money to help those that truly need it. Our church is only one in Memphis. There are many more. The Fathers House is a ministry that helps guys out of prison with the transition.

Jesus has a special heart for those who are weak and hurting, Kids, Widows, Poor, and Sick. If we want Jesus' heart, we need to look at the weak and see them as he does. This doesn't have to be an everyday thing. But look for an opportunity to help. Volunteer a couple times a year to help a big push to help a lot. You could do a once a month small outreach, or get into a Mentoring Program. I volunteer twice a month to mentor in the inner city. That doesn't make me better; it only means I make myself available for service. Anyone can do that.

Key; doing something for someone that isn't in the position to do something back to you.

Doing something for nothing.

Day 115

Matthew 26:1 & 2 – Doing Something for Nothing

His Crucifixion is only a couple days away. Remember Jesus did not get caught by surprise. He did not get tricked. He knew exactly what was coming. He also didn't leave the disciples unaware, though they didn't listen very well. He had to tell them several times before it started to sink in. Even then it was just hard to believe. Jesus could get away. He always knew what the enemy was thinking. They knew he couldn't be tricked. He could walk away on water if he had to, probably fly if he desired.

Jesus wanted to make sure they were ready, for they would soon be on their own.

Point: Jesus may not give us all the information up front, but he will not lead us blindly. He leads us into the unknown enough to build our faith and to give us a chance to show it. But at the same time he gives us hints. Along with the hints he gives us confirmations of the direction he is leading. This Sunday was the first time to visit The Springs, after we felt the call to move out there. I can't put it into words, but God gave us the confirmation we needed. When it was time to leave to get back to Raleigh to set up for class (I still had to teach my current class), it was so hard to get up and leave. I wanted to stay. I felt like I was at home. Each room was new and unfamiliar, but it was filled with potential and ideas. God revealed to me that the plan he has for me is real. He confirmed that the move to The Springs is the direction he wants me to go. I don't know what I will teach the first Sunday, or even the order of service. But I will be there, ready to serve.

God has kept us alive not to drag out our miserable life, but so we can find the Joy of serving. Yes the Joy of serving. The Joy comes from giving love to those who need it most. For me it's the kids. I want the kids to know just how much Jesus loves them before life without Jesus builds up so much hardness in their heart, they are lost forever.

What is God leading you to do?

Day 116

Matthew 26:10-13 – Don't Be Afraid to Follow

This is the story of the women that poured oil on Jesus' feet. She was preparing his body for burial. But what I see in this is the fact that once again the ones who are suppose to know what's going on. The ones, who have spent 3 years with Jesus himself, miss it once again. The woman was doing just as she was directed, by the Holy Spirit. Yet, instead of the disciples praising her faith, they condemn her.

Today while we have the Holy Spirit to guide us and to give us clarification, many still only see what they want to see. They only care about what effects themselves instead of the body of Christ. I am blessed to have friends that have been very supportive in all of my ministries. Even when God is doing great things, there are still those in the church that will get mad.

Even though some may appose you, and even though some of those that come against you may be Christians that have been in your church for years, it doesn't mean they are right.

Follow the Holy Spirit not Man. God will use man to give you confirmation and it will be a peace that comes from what they say. When you are feeling the leading of Jesus and someone gives you a message that is the opposite, and brings a bad feeling. This does not mean you are in the wrong. They most likely are not giving you a message from the Lord. It may sound right, but when the right message comes along, you will find peace in it. **The Holy Spirit is a peace giver**.

Follow the Spirit and listen to your friends, but remember your friends aren't smarter than God. Always side with God and the end results will be perfect. Live for God and Live forever. Live forever in a manor that is pleasing to God. Expect opposition, it just may be a sign you are on the right track.

The Devil doesn't want you to do well.

Day 117

Matthew 26:36-39 – Blood and Pain

Here we find Jesus in the garden with Peter, James, and John. We see Jesus grieving. He knew the ultimate results and that he would defeat death. But here he is just hours away from the punishment he knows full well is coming. He's begging his closest friends to sit with him. He can't stop thinking about the crucifixion, the whip, and the pain. Just a few verses back he reminds the disciples that he is not only the Son of God, but he is the Son of Man. Very much human. He will feel the pain, just as any man. The pain is very real.

The next day will find him beaten and killed in one of the worst methods in history. This was not a day he would be excited to get to. But at the same time, it was the very reason he came to earth. In his agony, he still cries out to God, not only looking for a way to avoid it, but ends it with, "Your Will."

He knew very well his blood was the only way that we could be washed clean. The only way we can get to heaven and be reunited with the Father.

The only way.

If it wasn't the only way, Jesus wouldn't have had to die, nor would he. Salvation has nothing to do with what we can do, but everything to do with God's grace and Jesus blood.

Jesus as a man still submitted to God the Father, when he knew it was going to be hard. He submitted to God's Will, even when it was going to be painful.

Can we follow and submit to God's Will when it is a bit on an inconvenience? What about when it is out of our comfort zone? Most likely we will not have to die to fulfill God's will. Remember when it gets a little tough; God's will always has a great ending. The pain will be worth it.

Day 118

Matthew 26:50 – Turn to Jesus

Here Jesus is tracked down by Judas, the Leading Priests, and a crowd of men with clubs. Jesus wasn't hiding. Jesus wasn't going to run. Jesus wasn't surprised. Of course this is when Judas gives Jesus a kiss to show the crowd which one was Jesus. That is actually in here.

Jesus addresses him as friend, not because he thought Judas was glad to see him, but because he really was a friend. Jesus picked him to be a Disciple. This means he was with Jesus for over 2 years and helped Jesus in many ways. He was not a clear betrayer. When Jesus first mentions that one of them would betray him, none of them knew or even had a clue, which it could be. So I'm sure the other eleven were surprised when Judas actually showed up with the crowd. If they had any clue before hand I'm sure Peter would have messed him up.

Jesus wasn't surprised. He knew exactly what Judas was there for. Jesus then tells him to go ahead and do it. He doesn't run. He doesn't fight. Jesus knew exactly what was about to happen, because it was the whole reason he came to earth. He went along with the crowd.

We know that later Judas hangs himself. This is sad, because Jesus would have forgiven him if he had asked. Jesus died even to cover the sin of betrayal. But without repentance, we are left with no hope. No hope all too often leads to suicide.

Suicide is not the way to handle guilt or loneliness. Turning to Jesus is.

Jesus can heal the hurt. He gave himself up to this crowd to be killed so we can be free from guilt, pain, hurts, and sin. Don't let this sacrifice be for nothing.

Call on Jesus and let him change your life. It is why he died.

The good news is he rose again.

Day 119

Matthew 26:64 – For the Good

Jesus is before the council. He lets them rant and rave for a while not saying a word. I'm sure this only infuriated them even more. He wouldn't answer their questions. They were trying to get him to say he was the Son of God. He never actually says it, but what he does say, is in some ways the opposite. He claims to be the Son of Man. Funny thing is so are they. He then adds that he'll be sitting beside God in heaven. He claims to be the messiah without actually saying it out right.

For two years the Pharisees and other religious leaders did not understanding a single word he said. They missed almost every hint or point Jesus made as they followed him around the country. Now they finally get it for the first time, with this one statement the Priests went nuts. They tore their clothes and shouted "Blasphemy!"

Jesus always knows exactly what to say and when to say it. He had to get them mad enough so they wouldn't back down, from the task at hand. Because Jesus had to die.

He needed Judas to betray him and now he needed the priest to lose it and force the Romans into killing him.

We can be used for good or evil. Follow the Holy Spirit, Read the Bible and let it be for the good.

Day 120

Matthew 28:20 – Be a Disciple, Don't Go it Alone

The great commission is for all of us to spread the good news of the gospel; I'm going to skip that today. Verse 20 takes it a step farther. This command isn't just for Peter, James, and John. It still applies to us today. This is why I write this devotional each day. I want to make sure you understand God's commands so you can obey them. You are his disciples and you too, need to share it with others. As we do this, Jesus will be with us today and tomorrow.

We need to study so we can be better disciples ourselves, and we need to do our best to help others to be good disciples and grow. Growing together is always better than growing alone.

The disciples had each other. Jesus always had them around, and even when he went to pray, he often took at a minimum of Peter James and John. Jesus didn't go through life alone, and he didn't need anyone's help. So shouldn't we do the same?

Jesus had them with him to teach them.

We need people with us to teach them, but also to learn from. Leave what you've learned with others and you will out live your own life.

Don't go it alone. Be a disciple. Disciples never go it alone. I don't think you can call yourself a disciple if you don't have others with you.

So as this book comes to a close please know; while every word, may have not been for you, it could be for someone you know. The Word of God isn't just for you, but it is for you to share.

Go and Share it.

Matthew – Jesus Speaks

Made in the USA
Charleston, SC
06 February 2013